Berlitz

KT-568-132

STOCKHOLM

- A ✔ in the text denotes a highly recommended sight
- A complete A–Z of practical information starts on p.99
- Extensive mapping throughout: on cover flaps and in text

14th edition

Although we make every effort to ensure the accuracy of the information in this guide, changes do occur. If you have any new information, suggestions or corrections to contribute, we would like to hear from you. Please write to Berlitz Publishing at the above address.

Text:	Edward Maze
Editors:	Peter Duncan, Alex Gray
Photography:	Jon Davison
Layout:	Suzanna Boyle
Cartography:	Visual Image

Thanks to: The Stockholm Information Service, Åke Lindström of AB Storstockholms Lokaltrafik, and Camilla Elvljung of the Swedish Travel and Tourism Council, for their invaluable help in the preparation of this guide.

Front cover: *Riddarholmen*
p.4 photograph: *Riddarholmskyrkan's lattice spire*

CONTENTS

The City and its People

Stockholm is widely acknowledged as one of the world's most beautiful cities. Dramatically situated at a point where the cobalt blue of Lake Mälaren meets and clashes with the darker hue of the Baltic Sea, the city has been splendidly endowed by nature. It sprawls gracefully over 14 islands connected by no fewer than 40 bridges. Swedish novelist Selma Lagerlöf described Stockholm most aptly as 'the city that floats on water'.

Stockholm had to wait almost 400 years before becoming Sweden's capital in 1634, and even then growth was painfully slow until the middle of the 19th century. Now the city is not only the seat of the national parliament and of the royal palace, but also the country's financial and business centre. Whilst there is plenty of elbow room in Sweden – the fourth largest country in Europe – more than one-sixth of the total population (about 8.5 million) crowds into the Stockholm area.

In recent decades, an ambitious building programme has added a whole new aspect to the 700-year-old city. In the centre, classic towers and turrets have given way to buildings with roofs as flat as pancakes, and offices have replaced apartments, forcing many former residents out to the mushrooming suburbs.

Stockholm's new architecture is most in evidence at Sergels Torg, named after the 18th-century Swedish sculptor Johan Tobias Sergel. Today the artist, who had a studio near here, would scarcely recognize the place. This square is the focal point of modern Stockholm, sporting a multi-million dollar shopping mall. It has become the city's main protest centre, where speakers rage against the tyranny of foreign dictators, cry out in favour of gay rights and women's lib, demand more day-care centres for tots, and so on, in an often carnival-like spirit. In atmosphere as much as architecture, **5**

Segels Torg epitomizes the spirit of modern Sweden.

And yet, there are also green parks and flower-filled squares, church steeples silhouetted against a mauve midsummer sky, narrow lanes and wide quayside boulevards for strollers, billowing sailboats and motorboats dotting the channels and the archipelago, which starts at the city's doorstep. The different islands and districts that make up Stockholm are often so unlike one another that they create the illusion of a series of miniature and only distantly related cities. Each has its own **6** distinct charm and mood.

Take Gamla Stan, the Old Town, for instance. In this island of antiquity in the heart of the city, Stockholm first saw the light of day around 1252. Strolling along its many cobbled alleys and twisting lanes, flanked by perfectly preserved 15th- and 16th-century houses, some with copper roofs, takes you back to medieval times.

By way of contrast, Norrmalm, the northern sector of town and location of Sergels Torg, represents the world of the late 20th century – the glass skyscrapers, shopping malls, underpasses, overpasses and traffic circles of the city centre. Adjoining Norrmalm is

Östermalm, a highly fashionable neighbourhood consisting of stately apartment buildings, where many of the city's foreign embassies are located.

Kungsholmen, the island just west of the city centre, hosts the municipal administration. The area is graced by the strikingly handsome Stadshuset (City Hall), rising on the shore of Lake Mälaren.

For another face of Stockholm have a look at Söder, the huge, hilly southern island overlooking the rest of the city. Its lofty location and numerous artists' studios give Söder a kind of Montmartre atmosphere. Here you'll find charming clusters of old wooden cottages in rural-like settings.

Stockholm spends a great deal of money on beautifying the city and maintaining its extensive recreational areas. One million flowers are planted every year in the municipal parks, which also have 150 playgrounds for children and as many as 30 open-air stages where ballet, drama, band concerts and folk dances are presented free of charge during summer. More than 500 sculptures adorn parks and squares all over town.

Cultural life in Stockholm thrives as never before, in particular the performing arts, which receive large national and municipal subsidies. Public money supports the 200-year-old Royal Opera, one of the best in the world, as well as the excellent Royal Dramatic Theatre. The city also boasts over 50 museums.

Stockholm can perhaps lay claim to having the world's most extensive art gallery: the

Stockholm's spectacular summer water festival is one of the city's great summer attractions. **7**

underground transport system, which stretches over almost 100km (60 miles). The walls and ceilings of many of its stations are decorated with paintings, stone and inlaid glass mosaics, sculpture and other art forms. It's worth a ride on the underground for this experience alone.

At one time nightlife was almost non-existent in Stockholm, but along with the new architecture came a virtual explosion of nightclubs, pubs and discotheques, and the city now swings after dark. Eating habits have also changed, with foreign cuisine – Chinese, French, Italian and others – replacing traditional Swedish food in many restaurants. This culinary switch is due in part to the great influx of foreign workers into the country, but also to the fact that Swedes, who enjoy at least five weeks' fully paid vacation each year, are travelling abroad in increasing numbers and acquiring new tastes in food.

A glance at shop windows or people on the street confirms that this is a very affluent city. Stockholmers live well and dress well. In the stores you'll find the best of Sweden's famous design products, including superb crystal from the glassworks district of Småland in the southeast part of the country.

What about the Swedes themselves? One could generalize by saying they are a very pragmatic, orderly and perhaps overly reserved people with a strong sense of social consciousness. They have put many innovative, humane laws on the books that have become models for the world. If the Swedes appear to be very materialistic, they also remain close to nature. The average Swedish home may be over-equipped with kitchen gadgets, but come summer, the family retreats to its modest *stuga*, or cottage, amid rustic woodland for a taste of the simple life. From July to September, armies of berry pickers and mushroom hunters invade the forests.

As a summer city, Stockholm – and especially its lovely environs – is hard to beat.

Tourist sightseeing boats glide under the bridges, and white steamers sweep through the wonderful island labyrinth of the Baltic archipelago or head for Drottningholm and Gripsholm, two marvellous palaces on the outer shores of Lake Mälaren. There are music and dancing in the city parks, concerts at the Royal Palace, recitals in many of the museums and churches; and much of the city – water, bridges, squares, steeples – is bathed in the eerily beautiful midsummer light.

Nevertheless, Stockholm is well worth visiting at other times of the year as well. There are some people who admire it most when newly coloured leaves turn Strandvägen into an avenue of autumn glory, or when the buds burst violently in Haga and other parks in the spring. Few would deny the enchanting beauty of the city in the dead of winter, when snow makes picture-postcard scenery out of narrow lanes and tiny squares, and bays, channels and canals freeze over solidly, allowing Stockholmers to walk and ski over the waterways and inlets of the sea. It is fair to say that the spectacular, seasonal transformations belong to the experience of Stockholm just as truly as its architectural juncture of old and new.

So many of the events that take place in Stockholm's streets draw fascinated crowds.

A Brief History

Swedish history begins somewhere around 12000BC – at any rate, this is what archaeologists have established as the time when the miles-thick blanket of ice covering the whole country started to melt. In the subsequent millennia, nomadic tribes of hunters and fishermen followed the receding ice cap northwards to the area that is now Sweden. About 3000BC the inhabitants of the area were cultivating the land, raising livestock and living together in communities. Magnificent Bronze Age artefacts, including weapons and ornaments, indicate an early period of prosperity. Mysterious rock carvings of animals and people also survive from the pre-historic period.

History in the Field

Sweden's elongated landscape – stretching about a thousand miles from north to south – can be compared to a vast open-air museum with fascinating artefacts from the dim past.

Foremost are the Viking rune stones, scattered throughout the country. These strange memorials record history and perpetuate myths. Their hieroglyphics and picture-writing recount the ancestry, the everyday and heroic moments of the Viking warriors for whom the rune stones were raised. A fine selection are on display in Historiska Museet in Stockholm (see p.49).

Other features of the landscape dating from far-off times include cromlechs (stone burial enclosures), fabulous rock carvings of boats, animals and people, and Viking burial mounds.

Best of all, perhaps, are Sweden's lovely medieval country churches. Filled with remarkably well-preserved naïve wood sculptures, stained glass windows, altar paintings and murals, they form an integral part of the countryside.

By the time that Swedes, however, are mentioned for the first instance in recorded history, conditions had altered substantially. This was in AD98, in *Germania*, where Roman historian Tacitus described the *Sviones*, or Svear tribe, as fierce warriors with mighty fleets. They were based around Lake Mälaren, gradually rose to a position of dominance over the neighbouring tribes, and in their seafaring exploits heralded the start of the Viking Age (AD800-1050).

The Vikings

The Vikings are best remembered for their ferocious raids on countries that were better off. They simply helped themselves to what they wanted rather than eke out an existence in their harsh homeland. Some of the battles and exploits of this time are recorded on the thousands of rune stones to be found in Sweden.

However, the popular image of the Vikings as the villains in history has been undergoing revision. Modern scholarship

A rune stone, inscribed with the marks of the Viking age, stands in a Stockholm park.

has revealed that the Vikings were also remarkable poets and artists, explorers and settlers who made many positive contributions to the territories they occupied. In their famous long ships, manned by as many as 50 oarsmen, these extraordinary seamen pushed west to England, Ireland and Scotland, then overran large areas of France, established new colonies in the Faroes, **11**

This wooden sculpture from the wreck of the Wasa is now on display at the Vasamuseet.

Iceland and Greenland, and finally reached the shores of North America. And those Swedish Vikings, who turned towards the east, travelled along the rivers of Russia, establishing control over Novgorod and Kiev, and went on as far as Constantinople.

The Vikings' navigational skills also equipped them admirably for far-flung trading expeditions, and they became merchants as well as marauders. For commercial reasons these heathens turned to religion to improve their dealings with Christian countries.

Early Christianity

Throughout the Viking period, Christian missionaries, mostly English and German monks, were active in Sweden. The first Christian church was founded about 830 in Birka by Ansgar, a monk from Picardy.

Christianizing Sweden was an uphill battle, to say the least, and there were sporadic lapses into paganism as late as the 12th century. In Uppsala, for instance, yearly sacrificial feasts were held in honour of the Norse gods. By the 13th century, however, the Church had become a dominant force in the country. The first archbishop, with a diocese in Uppsala, was appointed in 1164, and many churches were built during this period.

Historical Landmarks

AD98   First mention of the *Sviones* in Tacitus' *Germania*.

800-1050 Swedish Vikings raid and explore overseas.

830   First Christian church founded on Birka, a small island in Lake Mälaren.

1160   St Erik, Sweden's patron saint and king, dies.

1164   First archbishop appointed, in Uppsala.

1252   Founding of Stockholm by Birger Jarl, on the island known as Gamla Stan, the Old Town.

1477   Uppsala University, the oldest of Sweden's six universities, is founded.

1520   The Scandinavian monarch, Christian II of Denmark, executes some 80 Swedish noblemen in the Old Town during the 'Stockholm Blood Bath'.

1523   Gustav Vasa, founder of the modern Swedish state, reclaims Stockholm and gives the city stature as 'the head and lock of the entire country'.

1634   New constitution is adopted, and Stockholm officially becomes the capital of Sweden.

1654   Queen Kristina converts to Catholicism and announces her abdication in a speech at Uppsala Castle.

1792   Gustav III is assassinated at a masked ball in the Stockholm Opera House.

1901   First Nobel prizes awarded in Stockholm.

1912   The Olympic Games are held in the newly built Stockholm Stadium; the playwright August Strindberg dies.

1923   Stockholm's famous City Hall is inaugurated.

1950   Gustav V dies in Stockholm at the age of 92, ending a reign of 43 years.

1986   Swedish prime minister Olof Palme is mysteriously shot and killed by a gunman in Stockholm.

1994   Sweden decides by referendum to enter the European Union.

During the 13th century, a time of strife and contending factions, one important figure to emerge was Birger Jarl. Brother-in-law to the king, he promoted the idea of a strong central government and encouraged trade with other nations. When the king died,

*O*ne of Stockholm's more colourful citizens, a Laplander engaged in traditional craftmaking.

Birger Jarl had his own son elected heir to the throne. He is also credited with founding Stockholm, in about 1250, as a fort to protect against pirates.

The outstanding personality of the following century was St Birgitta, a religious mystic. Born in 1303, this remarkable woman was a prominent court figure, wife of a nobleman and mother of eight children. She founded a monastic order and church in the town of Vadstena in central Sweden, and her book *Revelations*, translated into Latin and widely read in the Christian world, is considered a masterpiece of medieval literature. St Birgitta died in Rome, but her remains were brought back to Vadstena and buried in the church there.

The Kalmar Union

To counteract the rapidly increasing power of the German Hanseatic League of the time, the so-called Kalmar Union was formed in 1397. It united Sweden, Denmark and Norway under a single ruler, the very able Queen Margareta of

Denmark, making it Europe's largest kingdom.

The Swedes came, in time, to resent the dominance of the Danes and many were opposed to the union. In the 1430s they were led in a popular rebellion by the great Swedish hero Engelbrekt, who also assembled the first Swedish parliament in 1435. This *Riksdag*, which included representatives of the four estates – nobles, clergy, burghers and peasants – elected Engelbrekt regent of Sweden. Soon afterwards he was murdered and the unpopular union limped along until 1520.

In that year the Scandinavian monarch, Christian II of Denmark, ruthlessly executed scores of Swedish noblemen, opponents who had been accused of heresy. However, instead of eliminating revolt, the 'Stockholm Blood Bath' unleashed a popular reaction that led to the disintegration of the despised Kalmar Union.

One of the noblemen who escaped death, Gustav Vasa, called on the peasants of the province of Dalarna to rebel against the Danish tyrant. With a ragtag army supported by foreign mercenaries, he succeeded in routing the Danes. He was crowned king in 1523 at the age of 27, and his dynamic reign dominated the 16th century.

Gustav Vasa was a strong-willed leader who reshaped the nation, earning himself the sobriquet 'Father of His Country'. He reorganized the state administration and stabilized its finances by, among other things, confiscating all of the church's considerable property holdings. Three of his sons ruled Sweden after he died in 1560, and the Vasa dynasty survived for almost 150 years.

Sweden as a World Power

Foremost among the Vasa kings was Gustavus Adolphus, crowned in 1611 at the age of 17. He promoted trade and industry and extended the borders of Sweden by conquests in Russia and Poland. Under his leadership Sweden became, for a time, the greatest power in 17th-century Europe. **15**

However, it could be considered a portent of things to come that in 1628 the imposing warship *Wasa* (see p.36), a fitting symbol of a mighty nation, sank in the Stockholm harbour on her maiden voyage. A few years after this calamity, Gustavus Adolphus was killed in battle in Germany, defending the Protestant cause in the Thirty Years' War.

As his daughter Kristina was only six when Gustavus Adolphus died, the extremely capable Count Axel Oxenstierna served as regent. Kristina was crowned in 1644. A very gifted but eccentric woman, she made her court a brilliant salon, inviting to her capital famous European intellectuals such as the French philosopher Descartes. Stockholm began to

*S*tained-glass window commemorating two Swedish kings, Gustav Vasa and Oscar II.

evolve from a rustic village into an elegant city. Ten years later, however, the queen startled the nation by abdicating; she converted to Catholicism and settled in Rome.

During the 17th century Sweden (which had previously annexed Estonia) gained additional ground in the Baltic and along the German coasts, and extended its borders into parts of Denmark and Norway. Sweden also established its first colony in America, in what is now Delaware, which was later captured by Britain.

Sweden's final moments as a great power occurred under Charles XII, who became monarch of the realm in 1697 at the age of 15. He is one of the most celebrated and controversial figures in the history of Sweden. Encouraged by a series of brilliant victories on the battlefield, the young king led his army deep into the interior of Russia in 1708-9. There he met with a disastrous defeat at Poltava in the Ukraine.

After an extended exile in Turkey, Charles XII took up arms once more and was killed in Norway in 1718. Among historians there has been considerable debate as to whether the fatal bullet came from the enemy or from one of the king's own soldiers.

In any event, his death marked the end of Sweden's Baltic empire. Only Finland and part of Pomerania remained. Decades of unremitting warfare left the country weak and in debt.

The Golden Age

The years of peace that followed were a Golden Age of culture and science in Sweden. During this period, Carolus Linnaeus laid the foundations for modern botanical science by classifying the flora of the world; Anders Celsius, the physicist and astronomer, developed the centigrade thermometer using a scale of 100 degrees between the freezing and boiling points of water; and Emanuel Swedenborg anticipated the findings of modern scientific research in a remarkable number of ways, and founded a new church.

Culture flourished during the reign of Gustav III (1771-92). The king, an ardent supporter of music, literature and art, founded the Royal Opera and the Swedish Academy to counter French influence and encourage the Swedish language. (The Academy awards the Nobel Prize for Literature.) He also gave the nation what is known as the elegant 'Gustavian' style, the local version of Louis XVI style.

However, Gustav III was mortally wounded in an assassination attempt at a masked ball in the Stockholm Opera House, and Sweden was subsequently drawn into the Napoleonic wars. In 1809 Finland, which had been a part of

The Pacifist who Invented Dynamite

Alfred Nobel (1833-96), inventor, engineer and industrialist, held more than 350 patents during his lifetime. While still in his teens he became a first-rate chemist.

The paradox is that Nobel, a pacifist at heart, should have invented dynamite, which proved such a boon to modern warfare. He also patented blasting gelatin, a substance more powerful than dynamite, and invented smokeless gunpowder. These products formed the basis of his industrial empire, which spread across five continents.

Nobel established the celebrated prizes in his will, drawn up a year before his death. They were to go to those who 'shall have conferred the greatest benefit on mankind' with the stipulation that 'no consideration whatever shall be given to the nationality of the candidates'. His entire fortune, which amounted to many millions of dollars, was used for this purpose.

First awarded in 1901, Nobel prizes fell into five categories: physics, chemistry, medicine or physiology, literature, and achievements in the cause of peace.

Sweden for 600 years, was possessed by Russia under an agreement between the czar, Alexander I, and Napoleon. Within quite a short time, the Bernadotte dynasty was 'imported' from France. A field marshal under Napoleon, Jean Baptiste Bernadotte was elected to the Swedish throne (as Karl XIV Johan) in the hope of obtaining French assistance in recovering Finland. In the event, Sweden participated in a final offensive to defeat Napoleon, with whom Denmark was allied. One of the results was Denmark's cession of Norway in 1814. The latter remained attached to Sweden until 1905.

An agricultural crisis hit Sweden towards the end of the 19th century. The hard times caused hundreds of thousands of Swedes to emigrate to America in the 1880s. Nevertheless, far-reaching social and political changes in Sweden improved life in many ways for those who decided to stay at home. Among other things, the four-estate parliament was supplanted by a two-house version. (The latest development occurred in 1971, when parliament was reduced to a single house.)

The 20th Century

The 20th century saw Sweden shifting rapidly from a farming economy to an industrial one. More and more people moved from rural areas to towns and cities. And the emigration to America also continued, so that by 1930 about a million Swedes (one out of five) had settled in the New World.

At the same time, the power of the labour unions and their ally, the Social Democratic Party, founded in 1889, was increasing. Hjalmar Branting, the great socialist leader, became prime minister in 1920, setting the stage for vast social reforms that were to make Sweden the world's leading welfare state.

Swedes may pay the highest taxes in the world to support cradle-to-grave security, but most of them feel they get a lot in return for their money – in the form of housing subsidies, **19** maternity leave, child allowances, free hospital care, old-age pensions and a host of other benefits. These and other social measures in operation, however, fall far short of classic socialism, and the bulk of Swedish industry is still controlled by private interests.

The solid success of Swedish industry, in fact, has not only made the welfare state possible, but also helped to give the Swedes one of the world's highest standards of living. The nation has been able to exploit effectively its few natural resources, namely iron ore and timber.

The technical genius of the Swedes played a significant role in building an affluent society, too. Many of Sweden's international companies have been developed on the basis of Swedish inventions such as dynamite (invented by Alfred Nobel – see p.18), the modern calculator (Odhner) and the important three-phase alternating electrical current system (Jonas Wenström).

Innovations in many fields, from sex education in schools to urban planning, have resulted in Sweden being looked upon as a kind of 'model country'. Sociologists, architects, educators and other specialists have come in great numbers to learn what they can from the Swedish experience. Sweden has also been a pace-setter in applied arts, and for many years the expression 'Swedish Modern' was virtually a synonym for good design.

Sweden remains a constitutional monarchy with the king as head of state, but actual power rests solely with parliament, one of the oldest legislative bodies in the world. The Social Democrats, who held office for a record 44 years before losing power for a brief spell between 1976 and 1982 to a coalition of non-socialist parties, have been the dominant factor in 20th-century Swedish politics. Nonetheless, the country has mostly been governed by consensus, with decisions reached by discreet compromise. All of the nation's political parties have supported the broad outlines of the welfare state.

The 20th century has been a time of almost uninterrupted stability and peace for Sweden. It fought its last war in 1814, and adopted a policy of strict neutrality that kept it out of both world wars.

Even the unexplained assassination of the Social Democratic Prime Minister, Olof Palme, in 1986 failed to destabilize Swedish society, though it briefly shook the nation's self-confidence.

Notwithstanding their capacity for neutrality and compromise, Swedes are concerned to avoid isolationist policies. The country has supported the United Nations ever since its inception, and it voted in a 1994 referendum to join the European Union. Not about to rest on its laurels, the 'model country' is carefully looking to its future in Europe.

This charming two-horse carriage is just one of the various forms of transport in Stockholm.

What to See

Look at the map of Stockholm and what do you see? A lot of blue (water) and green (parks), many islands and bridges, and streets that appear to run in all directions without rhyme or reason. You can get a bird's-eye view of all this from the

A young Swede relaxing on a Stockholm quayside surveys the calm beauty of the water setting.

observation platform at the top of **Kaknästornet**, the tallest building in Scandinavia. The vista is stunning, an excellent visual introduction to Stockholm. You'll see at once that the city is beautiful, though its layout may also strike you as rather confusing.

Getting around Stockholm is not as difficult as you might think. Much of what you'll want to see is concentrated in and around Norrmalm, the city centre, and Gamla Stan, the Old Town. A good public transport system makes the other parts of the city easily accessible too.

As a starter, take a city **boat tour** from Strömkajen near the Grand Hotel, or from Stadshusbron (City Hall Bridge). A one-hour tour circles the island of Djurgården, Stockholm's biggest park area, while a two-hour excursion takes in both the Baltic Sea and Lake Mälaren sides of Stockholm. You glide under bridges and through narrow channels and canals, passing dockyards, apartment houses, quayside boulevards, castles and parks.

This is a great way to have fun, and an excellent way of capturing the feel of the city.

A number of Grand City bus tours cover much of the city; they depart from Gustav II Adolfs Torg in front of the Royal Opera House. Helpful multi-lingual guides point out and explain the sights of both the bus and boat tours.

Stockholm's trams, an attraction in themselves, travel the route from Norrmalmstorg to Waldemarsudde daily in summer (in winter, they operate on weekends only). You will need a 'special' ticket, which can be bought on the tram as you board. Though not as quaint a way to travel, the more extensive bus and underground system offers cheap one-day and three-day tourist tickets. The taxis, however, are very expensive.

Stockholm is a city for wandering around in. This is the best way for anyone to experience its multiple charms and moods. So, make sure you have comfortable shoes.

Stockholm Highlights

Gamla Stan (Old Town): historic heart of Stockholm spread across four small islands. (See p.30)

Kungliga Slottet (Royal Palace): remarkably open palace, with beautiful interior, fine Treasury and *Livrustkammaren*; changing of guard April-Oct Mon-Sat 12.15pm and Sun 1.15pm, Dec-May Weds and Sat 12.15pm, Sun 1.15pm. (See p.30)

Storkyrkan (Great Church): 13th-century church and site of numerous coronations. (See p.33)

Djurgården (Animal Park): former royal hunting park on unspoiled island, with museums and quiet coffee shops. (See p.36)

Vasamuseet, *Djurgården*: world's oldest identified ship, recovered from Stockholm harbour and restored. (See p.36)

Skansen, *Djurgården*: open-air museum, representing old ways of life in Sweden, with zoo and other outdoor attractions. (See p.39)

Stadshuset (City Hall): imposing landmark, with handsome interior Golden Hall and lofty tower giving views over city. (See p.42)

Millesgården, *Torsviks Torg*: home, studio and garden of famous sculptor Carl Milles, with works set in beautiful garden. (See p.44)

Skärgården (Stockholm Archipelago): 24,000 rocky islands offering opportunities for boat cruises, sailing, swimming, fishing or just plain relaxation. (See p.55)

Drottningholm Palace, *Lake Mälaren*: Sweden's Versailles, with gardens, Chinese Pavilion and 18th-century theatre. (See p.58)

Gripsholm Castle, *Lake Mälaren*: massive castle beside lake, housing fine collection of historical portraits. (See p.60)

Sigtuna, *Lake Mälaren*: lakeside idyll and Sweden's first capital, dating back to 11th century. (See p.62)

Skokloster, *Lake Mälaren*: well-endowed baroque palace with motor museum nearby. (See p.63)

Uppsala: riverside town boasting 500-year-old Uppsala University, 13th-century cathedral and fame as stamping ground of Swedish taxologist Linnaeus. (See p.64)

City Centre

You'll undoubtedly be spending a good deal of time in the New Stockholm, in Norrmalm, the city's northern sector. This is where the business, banking, shopping and entertainment facilities are concentrated, as well as the bigger hotels, the main city air terminal and the railway station.

Central Stockholm has been almost entirely rebuilt. You will see a bewildering array of shapes and materials characterizing the soaring towers of the new buildings. Old streets have been replaced by modern shopping malls with restaurants, cinemas and boutiques.

Your first objective should be to pay a visit to **Sergels Torg** (Sergel Square), focal point of the new city centre. It is marked out by a gigantic glass obelisk rising from a fountain right in the middle of a very busy traffic circle. The square's lower-level mall, built as a shopping centre, has become a gathering place for angry people, something like the speakers' corner of London's Hyde Park. Most protest marches start here.

This mall also serves as the entry to the great glass-fronted **Kulturhuset** (House of Culture), which attracts thousands of visitors daily. They come to see films and videos, to look at art and handicrafts exhibitions, to listen to music, poetry, dramatic readings and debates. Here, too, can be found the Stockholm Stadsteatern (Municipal Theatre), which stages both modern and classical plays in Swedish.

In Kulturhuset's innovative library you sink down in an easy chair fitted out with earphones and listen to an extensive selection of classical, pop or jazz music on records and tapes. There are private booths for recorded language study, foreign newspapers and periodicals and a special children's corner where the earphones broadcast fairy tales.

A short walk through a shopping mall, usually animated by the music and songs of street performers, will take you to **Hötorget** (Haymarket Square), the northern end of **25**

What to See

the row of glass skyscrapers that starts at Sergels Torg. Hötorget's open-air market, selling fresh fruit, vegetables and flowers, adds a touch of colour to the square. Also on Hötorget you will find **Konserthuset** (Concert Hall), a neoclassical building distinguished by an unusual façade of Corinthian pillars and bronze portals. The Stockholm Philharmonic Orchestra plays in this hall, where you can hear every kind of music, from chamber music to pop melodies. In front of the building you will see Carl Milles' **Orpheus Fountain**, one of the late Swedish sculptor's finest works (see p.44).

This striking iron sculpture harmonizes well with the modern Sergels Torg.

Double back to Sergels Torg, turn left, and you're on

26

Hamngatan, one of the main shopping streets. Its tenants include NK (short for Nordiska Kompaniet), Sweden's biggest department store, and newcomers like Gallerian, a covered shopping mall with many stores and restaurants.

At Hamngatan 27, **Sverigehuset** (Sweden House) will supply you information about Sweden. Inside is a regional tourist office, providing information on Stockholm and surrounding areas, as well as an exchange office, souvenir shop and bookshop. Tickets for the theatre, concerts and sports events can also be bought here.

Next door is Stockholm's liveliest park, **Kungsträdgården** (Royal Gardens), stretching from Hamngatan down to the waters of Strömmen. Established as a royal pleasure garden in the 16th century for the exclusive use of the court and the Swedish aristocracy, Kungsträdgården has now become a favourite gathering place for Stockholmers and visitors during the summer months. You will find cafés, open-air restaurants, botanical exhibits and statues lining the park. There is an outdoor stage for rock, chamber music and choral concerts. You can do just about anything in this park – take a folk dance lesson, watch a marionette show, play ping-pong or stand-up chess, ice-skate (in the winter), stroll under long rows of linden trees or simply relax on a bench and watch the crowd go by.

Continuing east on Hamngatan, you will pass the **Hallwylska Museet** at No. 4. This patrician mansion, built in the 1890s, contains 70 perfectly preserved rooms, crammed with Gobelin tapestries, china figurines, Flemish and Dutch paintings, antique furniture, assorted *objets d'art* and, in the library, a bowling alley. Further on, at Nybroplan, you will find the **Dramatiska Teatern** (Royal Dramatic Theatre), where such notable actors as Greta Garbo, Ingrid Bergman and Max von Sydow began their careers. Before his death in 1953, American playwright Eugene O'Neill bequeathed his last plays to the Dramatic Theatre, and their **27**

Finding Your Way

Knowing a few key geographical terms in Swedish may help unravel some of the enigmas of a strange city and help you to find your way around. You should note that the words for 'street', 'square' and so on are often tacked on to place names, as in *Skräddargränd* (Tailors' Lane). Here is a list of some of the most common ones you'll come across:

bro	bridge
gata	street
gränd	lane
hamn	port
holme	island
kyrka	church
ö	island
plan, plats	square
sjö	lake
slott	castle
stad	city
torg	square
väg	road

world premières, including that of *Long Day's Journey into Night*, were staged here. August Strindberg, a native Stockholmer, is frequently and splendidly performed, as are Shakespeare and other classics, and, of course, contemporary playwrights.

From Nybroplan walk along Nybrokajen, a quayside street facing a bay lined with boats. If you continue along the water's edge you'll soon reach **Nationalmuseum** (see p.46). Now head north, passing the Grand Hotel and the white steamers that go out to the Stockholm archipelago, then turn left at Arsenalsgatan, cutting through the lower end of Kungsträdgården.

On the way, note the statue of King Charles XII, Sweden's most celebrated historical figure, and further along, the 17th-century church **Jakobs Kyrka**. Pause a moment here to look at the marvellous portals, particularly the one on the southern side, which dates from 1644.

Up ahead is Gustav Adolfs Torg, a large square with an

equestrian statue of King Gustavus Adolphus, the Swedish hero of the Thirty Years' War. On the east side of the square you will see **Operan** (Royal Opera), which is housed in a sombre baroque-style building from 1898. King Gustav III, a great patron of the arts, founded the opera in 1773. It was here (in the original opera house) that he was shot and killed some twenty years later at a masked ball. Verdi, incidentally, used this drama as the basis for his opera *The Masked Ball*.

Swedes are proud of the Royal Opera's long and distin-

The white steamers anchored in front of the Grand Hotel cruise the Stockholm archipelago.

guished history. Some of the world's greatest singers – from Jenny Lind, the 19th-century 'Swedish Nightingale' who made a fabulously successful tour around the United States, to Jussi Björling and Birgit Nilsson – started here. This remarkable institution has a breathtaking output of nearly 400 performances of opera and ballet each season.

29

Gamla Stan

Stockholm's history is neatly concentrated in **Gamla Stan** (Old Town), known as the 'city between the bridges'. On this small island – actually four islands – in the heart of the city, Stockholm first flickered to life more than 700 years ago. The cobbled lanes and winding alleys of the Old Town follow the original medieval street plan. Its houses, palaces and soaring spires are steeped in history and you get the impression of being transported centuries back in time.

Exploring Gamla Stan is a must for every visitor to Stockholm. You can start from Gustav Adolfs Torg and cross over Strömmen, where the waters of the Baltic Sea and Lake Mälaren meet, on the gracefully arched bridge of Norrbro. On your right you have Riksdagshuset (House of Parliament) and ahead the massive façade of **Kungliga Slottet** (Royal Palace), dominating the northern end of the Old Town.

It *was* known as the biggest palace in the world still to be

inhabited by royalty (600 rooms), but the king and queen have now decided that Drottningholm is more suited to family life. The original Tre Kronor (Three Crowns) castle stood on the site here until it burned down in 1697. It was not until 1754 that the present building was completed – according to a design by Nicodemus Tessin the Younger, a notable court architect.

Kungliga Slottet is remarkably accessible to the public. Anyone can walk through the inner courtyard, and the main parts of the building are open to visitors. Be sure not to miss the beautifully preserved rococo interior of the Royal Chapel or Queen Kristina's silver throne in the Hall of State. The royal jewels are displayed in the **Treasury** and include the king's crown, first used for

This blissful Stortorget scene is a far cry from the day noblemen were gruesomely executed here.

Erik XIV's coronation in 1561, and the queen's crown, which was designed in 1751 for Queen Lovisa Ulrika, and is spectacularly studded with almost 700 diamonds.

31

*T*he royal family no longer re-sides in the Royal Palace, but the Royal Guard still does its duty.

Among other palace high-lights are **royal apartments** and galleries with magnificent baroque interiors, containing priceless 17th-century Gobelin tapestries, paintings, china, jewellery and furniture collec-**32** ted over the centuries by kings and queens. In addition to housing the Treasury (Skatt-kammaren), the palace con-tains three more museums. The **Palace Museum** in the cellar has artefacts from the Middle Ages; the **Museum of Antiquities** exhibits classical sculpture brought from Italy by King Gustav III during the 1780s; and the **Livrustkam-maren** is the Royal Armoury.

Formerly housed in the Nordic Museum, Livrustkam-maren is a fascinating collec-tion of the weapons and costumes of Swedish kings. Some of the more unusual ex-hibits you'll see include a stuffed horse ridden by Gus-tavus Adolphus when he fell in the Battle of Lützen in 1632, the uniform that Charles XII was wearing when he was fa-tally wounded in the trenches while besieging Fredrikshald, Norway, in 1718, and the cos-tume Gustav III had on when he was murdered at the Opera Ball, together with the assas-sin's gun and mask.

The **changing of the guard**, accompanied by music, takes place in the palace's outer

courtyard on Wednesday and Saturday at 12.15pm, Sunday at 1.15pm, and April-October weekdays at 12.15pm.

A gift shop is housed in the palace proper (see p.79).

Another place of interest in the immediate vicinity is **Storkyrkan** (Great Church), on Slottsbacken, diagonally across from the south façade of the Royal Palace. The city's oldest church (which dates from the 13th century) and the coronation site of most of Sweden's kings, Storkyrkan's dull baroque exterior gives no hint of the beauty of its late-Gothic interior. You should note the sculptural ensemble, *St George and the Dragon*, a 15th-century masterpiece exe-cuted by Bernt Notke, a wood-carver from Lübeck, which symbolizes Sweden's strug-gles to break free of Denmark.

Just a few steps from the church, in **Stortorget** (Great Square), a murderous event, which is known as the 'Stock-holm Blood Bath', took place in 1520. King Christian II of Denmark ordered some 80 Swedish noblemen beheaded here and their heads piled, pyramid-style, in the middle of the square. Among the fine old houses on Stortorget is **Börsen** (Stock Exchange), a handsome building dating from 1776. The Swedish Academy meets here to elect the Nobel Prize winners in literature.

What to do now? Actually, the best way to get the feel of the Old Town is to wander about aimlessly. There's some-thing to see or experience at every turn – antique shops housed in fine 15th- and 16th-century buildings, former mer-chant palaces, gabled houses decorated with ornate portals, and charming alleyways with quaint names like Gåsgränd (Goose Lane) and Skeppar **33**

Pedestrians barely have room to squeeze past one another on the Mårten Trotzigs Gränd.

Karls Gränd (Skipper Karl's Lane). You'll also come across many art shops and galleries, as well as smart boutiques selling trendy clothes, handcrafted jewellery and ceramics. Explore the Old Town haphazardly, by all means, but do be sure to include some of the spots mentioned below as you meander about.

Walk south along **Västerlånggatan**, just west of Stortorget; this is a long and gently curving medieval shopping street, entirely free of cars. When you finally reach Tyska

Brinken, make a short detour to the left and go to **Tyska Kyrkan** (German Church). It boasts a fine baroque exterior and opulent interior dating from the mid-17th century.

Continue along Västerlånggatan. Near the end on the left is **Mårten Trotzigs Gränd**, the narrowest street in Stockholm. This steep, lamplit stone stairway is scarcely more than a yard wide and takes you on to Prästgatan.

Västerlånggatan terminates at Järntorget (the Iron Market Square) and if you then swing around the square you will find yourself on **Österlånggatan**. This is another long winding street dotted with art galleries and craftsmen's shops. Like Västerlånggatan it stretches the length of the island, but is noticeably more tranquil.

Den Gyldene Freden (The Golden Peace) at Österlånggatan 51 near Järntorget is the most famous tavern in the Old Town. Its name comes from the Peace of Nystad of 1721, which marked the end of Charles XII's wars. The historic brick cellar rooms are associated with the 18th-century troubadour Carl Michaël Bellman, who dropped by here from time to time.

Walking north along Österlånggatan you pass by another statue of St George and the Dragon, as well as picturesque lanes with arched entrances to your right that run down to Skeppsbron quay. Österlånggatan takes you back to Slottsbacken and the Royal Palace.

From here, head west on Storkyrkobrinken until you reach a square called Riddarhustorget. This was where the assassin of Gustav III was brutally flogged before being beheaded. On the north side of the square is the classic 17th-century **Riddarhuset** (House of Nobility), perhaps Stockholm's most beautiful building. The original architect, Vallée, a Frenchman, was tragically stabbed to death in a dispute over the building plans, but a German, a Dutchman and then the original architect's son, Jean de la Vallée, completed the admirable redbrick and sandstone structure.

A stone's throw away across a bridge is the tiny island of **Riddarholmen** (Isle of the Nobility), closely linked to the Old Town. A Stockholm landmark dominates the isle – **Riddarholmskyrkan**, with its tall, distinctive cast-iron latticework spire. Founded as an abbey at the end of the 13th century, this church has been the burial place of Swedish kings for some 400 years.

Also on Riddarholmen are a former *Riksdag* building, several palaces and the coppertopped Birger Jarl's tower (see p.14), erected by Gustav Vasa in the 16th century.

At Riddarholmen quay you get a marvellous **view** of Lake Mälaren, the heights of Söder (southern part of Stockholm), and Stadshuset on Kungsholmen (see p.42). From here the striking City Hall building appears to rise straight out of the waters of Lake Mälaren.

Djurgården

It's not hard to see why Stockholmers just love Djurgården (which means 'Animal Park'). This is an immense, largely unspoiled island of natural beauty, which used to be a royal hunting park. In addition to miles of woodland trails and magnificent oaks, some of which go back to Viking times, it contains surprising statuary tucked away amidst its greenery, outdoor coffee shops and restaurants, and some of the city's principal museums.

Djurgården is perfect for picnicking, jogging, horseback riding or just enjoying a walk in quiet surroundings. One of the favourite promenades for strollers is along a path that winds and dips but never strays too far from the shoreline of Djurgårdsbrunnsviken, a lovely channel that merges with an even lovelier canal. In the winter, when the water freezes over, people skate or ski on the ice.

There are a number of ways to reach the western end of Djurgården, where the island's major attractions are grouped. From Gamla Stan you can take the ferryboat at the southern end of Skeppsbron quay – a short, delightful trip on a little steamer. From Norrmalmstorg you can take the tram. From central Stockholm there's the bus (No. 44 or 47). An even better alternative is to go on foot, starting at Nybroplan and then following **Strandvägen**, a fashionable quayside boulevard in the Östermalm section of town.

Whether you choose to walk along the central promenade lined with linden trees, or beside the quay, where the old schooners are anchored, you'll find this is a very pleasant stroll. Keep on Strandvägen until you reach Djurgårdsbron, the bridge to Djurgården. After crossing it, you will come to **Nordiska Museet**, which is a huge multi-towered building on your right (see p.49). Directly behind it you will find the **Vasamuseet**, where you'll see the world's oldest identified ship and Stockholm's number one tourist attraction, the restored *Wasa* warship.

This 17th-century man-of-war capsized and sank in the Stockholm harbour, only a few hundred feet from the spot where she was launched on her maiden voyage in 1628. There the *Wasa* remained forgotten, until 1956 when a marine archaeologist discovered her.

The salvaging of the *Wasa*, an incredible, almost miraculous, feat, has added a colourful chapter to the annals of Swedish maritime history. In addition to the well-preserved, and elaborately decorated hull, more than 24,000 items from the ship, including hundreds of wooden sculptures, have been recovered by divers who had to sift through some 40,000 cubic yards of mud in the *Wasa*'s grave.

During the lengthy restoration, experts were faced with the stupendous task of piecing together 14,000 fragments recovered from the deep. The completed *Wasa* was finally moved to her own permanent, spacious quarters on Galärvarvsvägen. In the open-plan museum, visitors can inspect her in her entirety on seven levels. Children will especially enjoy 'sailing' the *Wasa* using computer simulators.

Nearby are exhibition halls housing ornaments and other objects from the ship – pottery, coins, pewter tankards, glassware, clay pipes, cannon balls

The richly ornate hull of the Wasa *is one of the major highlights of the Vasamuseet.*

and items of clothing taken from the skeletons of 18 *Wasa* seamen found on the ship. Among the oddest discoveries were a box containing butter (rancid, of course) and a flask of rum, still drinkable after more than three centuries.

The best way of visiting the *Wasa* is to start by watching the introductory film (shown hourly) or take a guided tour (several times daily).

Further on, the **Biologiska Museet** lies to your left (see p.50). Follow Djurgårdsvägen until **Liljevalchs Konsthall**, which mounts excellent exhibitions of paintings, sculpture and handicrafts.

Only a few steps away is **Gröna Lund**, or Tivoli, Stockholm's amusement park. In addition to shooting galleries, a merry-go-round and a tunnel of love, it has a first-rate theatre and open-air stage, where top Swedish and foreign entertainers perform.

While you're in the area, pause to look at the cluster of old houses on some of the narrow streets near the amusement park. This community,

known as **Djurgårdsstaden**, was founded more than 200 years ago.

You should now cross over Djurgårdsvägen to reach the **Skansen** entrance, the world's first and most famous open-air museum, a prototype for all the others that followed. Beautifully situated on a 30ha (75-acre) hill, it was created by Artur Hazelius in 1891. The idea was to establish a kind of Sweden in miniature and show how people – from farmers to aristocrats – lived and worked during different eras.

Some 150 historic buildings from various parts of Sweden form the core of Skansen. They represent a bygone way of life, a culture that started disappearing with the advent of the Industrial Revolution. Gathered here are reassembled cottages, manor houses, peasant and Lapp huts and ancient farmsteads, which are complete with cows, pigs and other farm animals. Country stores and city shops, including a bakery and an old pharmacy, and the 18th-century Seglora Kyrka, popular for weddings,

Skansen attracts visitors of all ages in search of what life was once like in Sweden.

dot the area. Glassblowers, potters, bookbinders and goldsmiths are among the craftsmen plying their trade in the workshops. Tours leave from Bollnästorget in the summer.

Skansen has a zoo featuring northern animals such as reindeer, seals, wolves and deer, as **39**

The cable tram may be slow, but it is a relaxing way to travel to the Skansen open-air museum.

rants, public dance floors and an open-air stage.

There is always something going on and you can spend a whole day or more at Skansen without the risk of getting bored. The park is also a pleasant spot to visit in the evening – from the hilltop you see the city lights of Stockholm reflected in the water, sparkling in all directions.

Outside Skansen take bus No. 47 for a short ride to **Waldemarsudde** on the south shore of Djurgården. This is the former house and art gallery of Prince Eugen, who was widely known as Sweden's 'Painter Prince'. When he died in 1947 at the age of 82, he bequeathed his property to the nation. The public can visit both the house and the gallery in their lovely setting of parkland and terraced flower gardens stepping down to a channel of the Baltic Sea.

Waldemarsudde has an ambitious collection of Swedish paintings, mostly from the late 19th century. There are also more than a hundred works by Prince Eugen, who was a fine

well as fauna from other parts of the world. The park has a special children's area, Lill-Skansen, with rabbits, kittens, guinea pigs and other small animals, not to mention an aquarium, botanical gardens, **40** indoor and outdoor restau-

landscape painter as well as a collector of outstanding art. The garden contains a number of first-rate sculptures.

One other place worth visiting in Djurgården is **Thielska Galleriet**, an art gallery with a good collection of French and Scandinavian art. Of note are a group of engravings and paintings by the Norwegian Edvard Munch. There are also some works by August Strindberg, whose fame as a dramatist has tended to obscure his other talent as a painter. The gallery is housed in a Jugendstil building, which was commissioned by a wealthy banker, on the southeast end of the island. If you're energetic, you can walk there from Waldemarsudde. Alternatively, catch bus No. 69 from Norrmalmstorg in downtown Stockholm.

This period cottage interior, which you can see at Skansen, offers an insight into how some Swedes lived in the past.

41

Stadshuset and Other Sights

Most of the major points of interest are found in the areas covered thus far – Stockholm centre, the Old Town and Djurgården. However, there are a number of excellent attractions left to see. Foremost among these is **Stadshuset** (City Hall), which is located on Kungsholmen island west of the city centre. You can get there by crossing Stadshusbron (City Hall Bridge) from Tegelbacken.

When William Butler Yeats came to Stockholm in 1923 to receive the Nobel Prize for Literature, he took a look at the new City Hall and exclaimed that 'no work comparable in method and achievement has been accomplished since the Italian cities felt the excitement of the Renaissance …'

Yeats was not alone in lavishing praise on Stockholm's City Hall. Designed by Ragnar Östberg, the building rises gracefully and dramatically on the shore of Lake Mälaren. Artists and craftsmen from all over Sweden contributed to its creation, and it has become a fitting symbol, almost an architectural hymn, to the city.

Stadshuset is worth several hours of your time, and even then you'll only get an inkling of what went into the construction of this remarkable building. The special hand-cut brick façades, the imposing square

tower capped by three golden crowns, the black granite reliefs, pillars and arches – all miraculously blend together to form a unified and coherent whole, a monumental attempt to fuse together the many different elements that make up Stockholm.

Join one of the guided tours through the handsome interior

of the City Hall. Highlights include the **Golden Hall**, covered with striking mosaics, the huge glass-domed Blue Hall (which is actually red) where the Nobel Prize banquets are held, and the Prince's Gallery with its murals executed by Prince Eugen.

In the terraced garden by the water lie Carl Eldh's sculptures of the dramatist August Strindberg, the poet Gustaf Fröding and the painter Ernst Josephson. Also here, on top of a 14m (45ft) column, is Christian Eriksson's bronze statue of Engelbrekt, Sweden's great hero of the Middle Ages.

For a superb **view** of the Old Town and the central parts of Stockholm, go up to the top of the City Hall Tower.

Extending west of Stadshuset is **Norr Mälarstrand**, a landscaped promenade that

An aerial view from the tower of Stadshuset, showing the forecourt and terraced garden.

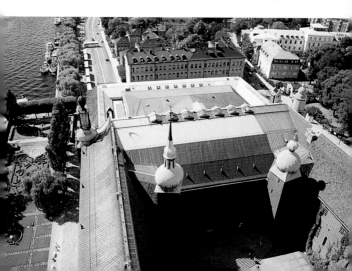

follows the water's edge all the way to the big Västerbron (Western Bridge). This pleasant walk is often crowded with Stockholmers out for a casual stroll and with parents pushing baby carriages, especially on a sunny Sunday afternoon.

One sight not to be missed is **Millesgården**, the home, studio and garden of the late Carl Milles, Sweden's famous modern sculptor. Although he lived and worked abroad for long periods, mostly in the United States, Milles was extremely fond of his place on the island suburb of Lidingö and managed to spend his summers here.

The gardens are beautifully terraced and overlook an inlet of the Baltic; they provide a superb setting for replicas of Milles' best work. On display are some of his most popular pieces – *Man and Pegasus, Europa and the Bull* and the spectacular *Hand of God*. There is also an important collection of Greek and Roman sculpture, as well as the work of other sculptors.

Millesgården itself is a work of art, the creation of a man who worshipped beauty. Silver birch and pine trees mingle naturally with statues and fountains, rose beds and urns of flowers blend with marble

One of Carl Eldh's sculptures stands prominently on the foreshore of Lake Mälaren.

columns and flights of lime-stone steps. Carl Milles died in 1955, at the age of 80, and both he and his wife are buried in a small chapel in the garden. Take the underground to Ropsten, then catch a local train to Torsvik or a bus (No. 201-206) to Torsviks Torg.

If you have enough time, go over to **Söder**, the large island on Stockholm's south side, with steep cliffs plunging down into the Baltic and Lake Mälaren. It's a place with a very special atmosphere, quite different from other parts of the city. Söder contains a number of small, closely integrated neighbourhoods, clusters of rust-red wooden cottages and artists' studios located in rural-like settings.

You should start at Slussen, a clover-leafed traffic circle above the narrow canal connecting the lake with the sea. In the summer months you'll see many pleasure boats lined up here, waiting for the canal lock to be opened.

Slussen is the site of **Stadsmuseum**, the Stockholm City Museum (see p.53). It is also home to one of the city's most curious sights – **Katarinahissen**, a lift that rises in an open shaft to the roof of a tall building. From the top you get a classic view of the Old Town. There is a gangway you can take to cross over to a clifftop neighbourhood of quaint old houses with hidden courtyards.

Now head for **Fjällgatan**, east of the Katarina district, where most of the city sight-seeing buses stop. This little street, perched along the edge of a towering ridge overlooking the Baltic, provides the visitor with one of the very best panoramas of Stockholm. Not far from here there is a charming colony of shuttered, fenced-in cottages grouped on the slopes of a grassy hill around the Sofia Kyrka.

To the west of Slussen, there are more picturesque houses at Mariaberget. From the heights of **Skinnarviksberget**, you will experience yet another stunning view of Stockholm, which will encompass sights of Lake Mälaren and Stadshuset. **45**

Museums

A number of important museums, such as Skansen, the warship *Wasa* and Millesgården, have already been covered. Here is a description of other major museums in Stockholm, including some of specialist interest. Opening hours may vary, so it is worth checking beforehand with the tourist office (see p.123).

 FIRST FIVE

Nationalmuseum (National Museum of Fine Arts)

Sodra Blasieholmen. Bus 43, 46, 55 or 62 to Karl XII:s Torg. This is one of the oldest museums in the world. It was opened to the public in 1794 and originally occupied a wing of the Royal Palace. The museum was moved to its present site, in an Italian Renaissance-style building, in 1866.

The collection is impressive, not only because of its size. Among the old masters **46** you'll find ten Rembrandts,

*B*ehind the striking façade of the Nationalmuseum are displays of Sweden's finest art treasures.

plus important works by El Greco, Rubens and Brueghel and a choice group of Chardin oils. Courbet, Cézanne, Gauguin, Renoir and Manet are represented, as are important Swedish artists, among whom are Carl Larsson, Anders Zorn and Bruno Liljefors (who is known for his vivid nature studies). Zorn's *Midsummer Dance* is a wonderful evocation of Midsummer's Eve in the province of Dalarna. Other paintings you should look out for include François Boucher's *The Triumph of Venus*, considered his greatest work, and *The Lady and the Veil* by the Swedish painter Alexander Roslin (1718-93). In addition to these special treats there are thousands of prints, engravings and miniatures, more than 200 Russian icons and a selection of handicrafts to appreciate. Open Wednesday-Sunday 10am-4pm, on Tuesday 10am-9pm; closed on Monday.

Moderna Museet (Museum of Modern Art)

Birger Jarlsgatan 57. Underground to Rådmansgatan or bus 46. With 'op', pop and all kinds of 'happenings', this stimulating, trend-setting institution has kept up with the best of contemporary art from the rest of Europe and the United States. The museum's extensive collection of 20th-century art includes works by Léger, Matisse, Braque, Modigliani, Klee and Rauschenberg, as well as by top Swedish artists such as Isaac Grünewald and Bror Hjorth.

The museum also offers music, film and theatre programmes, as well as changing exhibitions, in its impressive **Museum of Photography**, located in the building's western gallery. Open Tuesday-Thursday noon-7pm, Friday-Sunday noon-5pm; closed on Monday.

*P*icasso figures occupy an important place in the sculpture garden of the Moderna Museet. **47**

Östasiatiska Museet (Museum of Far Eastern Antiquities)

Skeppsholmen. Bus 46 to Karl XII:s Torg and then cross the bridge to the island. This enormous collection embraces art from Japan, Korea, India and China, from the Stone Age to the 19th century. The display of ancient Chinese art, considered the best in the world outside China, includes 1,800 objects bequeathed to the museum by the late King Gustaf Adolf VI, a distinguished ar-chaeologist and a respected authority on Chinese art.

The museum's star exhibits are numerous: Stone Age pottery from around 2000BC; a reconstructed Chinese grave furnished with urns and axe heads grouped around a skeleton; colourful ceramics dating from the Ming Dynasty (1368-1644); and a series of highly

The 19th-century schooner af Chapman is now a floating hostel outside Ostasiatiska Museet.

impressive bronze sacrificial vessels. Open Wednesday-Sunday noon-4pm, Tuesday noon-9pm; closed on Monday.

Nordiska Museet (Nordic Museum)

Djurgården. Bus 44 or 47. Hazelius, creator of Skansen, founded this museum illustrating life in Sweden from the 16th century to the present. As you enter the building you are greeted by Carl Milles' enormous oak statue of Gustav Vasa, father of modern Sweden (see p.15).

There is a lot to view here – more than one million objects, in fact. You'll find exhibits depicting the history of upper-class fashions, an interesting section on food and drink with table settings from different periods, and a costume gallery devoted to Swedish peasant dress from the first part of the 19th century. There's also a feature on the nomadic Lapps and their reindeer, and a section concentrating on Nordic folk art that includes Swedish wall paintings, Norwegian tapestries, Finnish drinking vessels and Danish embroidery. Open Monday-Friday 10am-4pm, weekends noon-5pm.

Historiska Museet (Museum of National Antiquities)

Narvavägen 13-17. Underground to Karlaplan or bus 44, 47 or 69. Ten thousand years of history are eloquently unfolded in this excellent museum. Before going inside have a good look at the main entrance. The 'door of history', covered with a multitude of allegorical and historical figures in bronze relief, is the work of the renowned Swedish sculptor Bror Marklund.

The museum has more than 30 rooms, so it's best to pick up a floor plan, available with explanations in English. The ground floor exhibits start with artefacts made by the earliest inhabitants of Sweden during the Mesolithic and Neolithic periods. The Viking Age has yielded a rich collection of gold and silver objects, fine examples of ornamental art, **49** and weapons and rune stones from the isle of Gotland. From a slightly earlier epoch, there is the Treasure of Vendel, a remarkable burial site with the dead in their boats surrounded by everyday objects.

Magnificent examples of medieval church art can be seen on the first floor. There are wooden crucifixes modelled after Byzantine art, beautifully painted and sculptured altar pieces, baptismal fonts, textile wall hangings, gold chalices and various processional crosses. One room has been given over entirely to a reconstruction of a typical medieval country church.

Kungliga Myntkabinettet (Royal Coin Cabinet) is on the second floor. Here on display is a fascinating collection of international medallic art from the 15th century to the present, as well as a massive collection of about 400,000 coins from all over the world, going back to 650BC.

Stockholm's major new attraction is the **Gold Room**, located in a 'rock chamber' **50** some 7m (23ft) below ground

level in the garden of Historiska Museet. The circular room displays one of Europe's richest collections of prehistoric jewellery, including gold and silver artefacts dating back as far as 400AD. Open Tuesday-Sunday noon-5pm, until 9pm on certain Wednesdays.

OTHER MUSEUMS OF INTEREST

Biologiska Museet (Natural History Museum)

Djurgården. Bus 44 or 47. Created in 1893 by two extremely talented men, the taxidermist Gustaf Kolthoff and the painter Bruno Liljefors, this admirable institution is said to have served as a model for New York's Museum of Natural History.

Here you can admire 300 different species of Nordic animals and birds, including polar bears, Arctic wolves, mountain hares and moose, hawk owls, white-tailed eagles and guillemots nesting on cliffs. They are stuffed, of course, but they look eerily real in these ingeniously constructed settings. The result is an absorbing museum that is sure to fascinate both children and adults. Open April-September 10am-4pm, October-March 10am-3pm.

Medeltidsmuseet (Museum of Medieval Stockholm)

Stockholm's most recent museum attraction, devoted to the city's medieval period, lies beneath the courtyard of the House of Parliament. On display you will find remnants of 13th-century fortifications and a section of the 16th-century town wall, which was accidentally uncovered by construction workers while excavating for the building of an underground car park.

This shell of a medieval sailing vessel is one of the fascinating displays at Medeltidsmuseet.

Naturhistoriska Riksmuseet (Museum of Natural History)

Frescativågen 40. Bus 40 and 540 or underground to Universitet. This huge museum was established in 1916 and covers various aspects of natural history, including specimens of birds and animals from the Arctic regions. The museum's biggest attraction is the new Omnimax Theatre, where a 70mm film frame is combined with a 180-degree fish-eye lens, which is the world's largest film format, to create spectacular images. The films shown are mostly documentaries, covering subjects like astronauts in space and unusual aspects of life on land and in the oceans. Open Monday-Sunday 10am-6pm, until 8pm on Thursday.

Postmuseum (Postal Museum)

Lilla Nygatan 6, in the Old Town. Bus 48 or 53 or underground to Gamla Stan. Documenting the history of the mail service in Sweden from its earliest days to the present, the museum contains an excellent philatelic department – in fact, it is one of the largest stamp collections for public viewing in the world. Among the rarities are the first English stamp cancelled on the day of issue, 6 May 1840. Open Monday-Saturday noon-3pm, and Sunday noon-4pm, and also in winter Thursday 7-9pm.

Sjöhistoriska Museet (National Maritime Museum)

Djurgårdsbrunnsvägen. Bus 69 from Norrmalmstorg. Located in a fine building designed by Ragnar Östberg, architect of the City Hall, this interesting museum traces the history of the Swedish navy and the merchant marine. The centrepiece of the collection is the stern of the schooner *Amphion*, which won a key naval battle against the Russian navy in 1790 under the command of Gustav III. Open daily 10am-5pm, and additionally in winter Tuesday 6-8.30pm.

Stockholms Stadsmuseum (Stockholm City Museum)

Slussen. Bus 43, 46, 48, 53, 55 or 59 or the underground to Slussen. Appropriately housed in the former 17th-century town hall, the museum carefully details the history of Stockholm. The exhibits include archaeological discoveries from the area, a fine model of the old Tre Kronor castle, paintings, sculptures from the façades of demolished buildings, and all kinds of objects used in the everyday life of the city. You can also enjoy coffee and snacks in the museum's charming 19th-century café, and there is even a play area for children. Open Tuesday-Thursday 11am-7pm, Friday-Monday 11am-5pm.

Strindbergsmuseet (Strindberg Museum)

Drottninggatan 85. The underground to Rådmangatan. The apartment in which Sweden's greatest playwright, August Strindberg, lived during the last years of his life has been reconstructed with authentic furnishings, including his original writing desk. Three adjoining rooms are devoted to his manuscripts, letters and photos of actors and actresses who appeared in his plays. Strindberg died in 1912. Open Tuesday-Saturday 10am-4pm, Tuesday 7-9pm, Sunday noon-5pm; closed on Monday.

Tekniska Museet (National Museum of Science and Technology)

Museivägen 7. Bus 69 from Norrmalmstorg. This museum covers Swedish science and technology through the ages. One of the great attractions is a reconstructed iron ore mine in the basement of the building. Another highlight is the Royal Model Chamber, displaying the inventions of Christopher Polhem (1661-1751), a genius described by many as the 'Father of Swedish Technology'. Open Monday-Friday 10am-4pm, weekends noon-4pm.

53

Excursions

The beauty of its surroundings more than match the beauty of Stockholm itself. To the east are the islands of the archipelago, and to the west is Lake Mälaren with a choice collection of castles and towns at the water's edge. The province of Södermanland, which is dotted with small lakes, churches and mansions, runs off from Stockholm's southern edge. And to the north there is Uppland, a province of prime historical interest, with hundreds of rune stones from the Viking Age.

There are plenty of boat excursions all summer long, on graceful old steamers or fast modern motor launches. Most of those heading for the Baltic islands will depart from either Norra Blasieholmshamnen or Strömkajen, both of them near to the Grand Hotel. Stadshusbron, next to the City Hall, is

*T*his ferry boat conveys commuters and tourists across the Strömmen every day.

the departure point for boats around Lake Mälaren.

You can also choose from a variety of bus tours, train excursions and some package trips that include an overnight stay in a hotel. The Stockholm Information Service can provide details (see p.123).

STOCKHOLM ARCHIPELAGO

The Swedes call the Stockholm archipelago Skärgården, which means 'garden of skerries'. It's a good description. Huge and infinitely varied, this garden consists of as many as 24,000 rocky islands of all shapes and sizes, extending for some 48km (30 miles) into the Baltic. There is nothing like it anywhere else in the world.

In its day the archipelago served as a place of refuge for pirates and smugglers. Later, fishermen lived in unpainted wooden shacks on many of the islands, and wealthy noblemen built great estates.

In this century the archipelago has become the favourite playground of Stockholmers who go to their summer holiday houses on weekends or for longer vacations. They sail and fish, swim and sun themselves while lying and sitting on the smooth boulders by the water.

The archipelago is divided into three distinct sections, each with its own character and special atmosphere. The inner group is made up of larger islands covered with forests and farmland. The middle archipelago consists of a jumble of large and small islands, some with woods and fields of wildflowers, separated by a labyrinth of narrow channels and sounds. Last, the outer archipelago, mostly uninhabited, is a barren seascape of desolate rock islands.

Less than an hour away by boat, **Vaxholm** is an attractive waterfront town in the inner archipelago. Its chief attraction is the 16th-century **Vaxholm fortress**, which used to guard the straits here and is now a museum, open on afternoons in summer.

Also worth visiting here is **Norrhamnen**, the old homestead museum. It is housed in **55**

*S*tockholmers relax amidst the beauty of Lake Mälaren, on their own doorstep.

two old buildings, the former homes of fishing families. Vaxholm has plenty of water-side strolling paths, and from the harbour you can watch the motorboats and sailboats manoeuvring through the narrow channel as they head for more distant points in the Stockholm archipelago.

Sandhamn is located on a Baltic island at the outer edge of the archipelago. The journey there takes three-and-a half hours by steamer – each with a restaurant on board – or two hours by motor launch. Either way you are able to take in all the diverse and dramatic elements that make up this stunning island world.

An important pilot station since the end of the 17th century, Sandhamn is a yachting centre and home of the fashionable Royal Swedish Yacht Club. The tiny, charming vil-

lage has only about 100 year-round residents. But the figure swells in the summer when tourists and Stockholmers who have summer holiday cottages there invade the island. Sand-hamn's summer amenities include several hotels, an old inn, a restaurant with dancing, and good swimming and sailing facilities. In July the island hosts an international regatta.

Within 30 minutes by train from Slussen, **Saltsjöbaden** is a posh suburb and resort area

in a lovely setting at the edge of the archipelago. Much of the activity here is centred around the Grand Hotel Saltsjöbaden, where you can eat and drink. Its range of outdoor activities includes swimming, sailing, tennis, riding and golf.

Tyresö Castle, 45 minutes by bus from Skanstull, sits on an inlet southeast of the city. This magnificent 17th-century country estate once belonged to Gabriel Oxenstierna, one of Sweden's leading noblemen.

Now a museum open to the public, its collections include some interesting period furniture and paintings.

Another enjoyable outing is across to one of Sweden's neighbours. Take a cruise to **Mariehamn**, the capital of the Åland islands – 9,970 square kilometres (3,850 sq miles) of bays, inlets, islands and skerries – located about midway between Sweden and Finland. This autonomous province of Finland has a population of **57**

20,000, most of whom also speak Swedish.

The day cruises leave in the morning, stop for a couple of hours in Mariehamn, and are back in Stockholm by late evening. You can also take a 24-hour excursion, sleeping on board in a comfortable cabin, or you can spend the night in a hotel in Mariehamn. The town has good accommodation facilities and a number of excellent restaurants.

Travellers on these cruise ships will enjoy a sumptuous *smörgåsbord*, and the bars, dance lounges and nightclubs on board are always lively. Tax-free prices make drinks during the journey inexpensive, and since the ships pass through the Stockholm archipelago you will enjoy a scenic feast as well.

LAKE MALAREN

Mälaren is the country's third largest lake, stretching out for more than 110km (70 miles) west of Stockholm. This area – the Lake Mälaren Valley – has been justly called the cradle of Swedish civilization. Its most important historic sights are within relatively easy striking distance of the city by road, rail or water.

As a starter, consider a trip to **Björkö** (Birch Island), one of the lake's 300 islands. This was the site of Birka, Sweden's earliest trading centre, where St Ansgar preached to the heathens in the year 830 and built a church. Obliterated in the 11th century, all that remains of the once flourishing town of Birka are the faint traces of old fortifications and something like 3,000 Viking graves. The island is a pleasant, relaxing place to spend part of a day. You can reach Björkö by boat in two hours, in summer only.

One of the most pleasant and rewarding excursions is to **Drottningholm Palace**, on a small island in an inlet of Lake Mälaren. A boat trip will take you through a beautiful stretch of Mälaren and will get you there in under an hour, or you can take the underground to Brommaplan and change to a bus marked 'Mälarö'.

A French-style palace, built in the late 17th century and described as the Versailles of Sweden, this is now the home of the royal family. Its formal gardens are big and impressive, with statuary, fountains, trees and lawns. Sections of the well-preserved interior – richly decorated with fine tapestries and other works of art – are open to the public.

The palace itself is open May-August every day 11am-4.30pm (from noon on Sundays) and during September daily 1-3.30pm.

Be sure to have a look at the **Chinese Pavilion** (Kina Slott), an unusual combination of the rococo and Chinese styles. It was constructed in the palace grounds in the 1760s as a gift to Queen Lovisa Ulrika.

Best of all is the **Drottningholm Court Theatre**, adjacent to the palace, one of the world's most famous theatrical establishments. This fully restored 18th-century theatre is unique in that its original sets (30 in all), stage machinery and props are in perfect working order and still in use. Except for the stage lighting – electricity has replaced candlelight – nothing has changed since King Gustav III, the patron of the arts, attended opera performances here.

During the summer months this gem of a theatre is the

*I*n a glorious setting of statuary, fountains and gardens, the royal residence, Drottningholm Palace.

venue for operas by Handel, Gluck, Mozart and others, as well as ballet. The additional touch of musicians dressed up in authentic period costumes and wearing powdered wigs makes you feel you're attending a court entertainment some 200 years ago.

Before or after the performance, take a chance to look at the collections of pictures and costumes tracing the history of stage art, which are exhibited in the rooms around the auditorium. They include rare Italian and French theatrical designs from the 16th to the 18th centuries and original sketches by Gustav III's stage painter.

Somewhere that justifies a full day's excursion is **Gripsholm Castle**, another of Lake Mälaren's outstanding attractions. You can get there in an hour and a half by train to

One of the massive turrets that make the 17th-century Gripsholm Castle so impressive.

Läggesta, and then a short bus ride. An alternative route, by boat, takes three-and-a-half hours, but is time well spent. The *SS Mariefred*, a coal-fired steamer that has been plying the same route since 1903, makes for a highly memorable trip. You can even enjoy a good dinner on board.

At journey's end you'll see Gripsholm's massive, turreted bulk mirrored like a stage set in the waters of the lake. There was a castle on this site in the 1300s, but the present structure was built by Gustav Vasa in the 16th century – and subsequently added on to and modified by just about every succeeding Swedish monarch. The castle served as a state prison at one time, and the deposed King Erik XIV was held captive in its tower.

Now a museum, Gripsholm houses one of the largest collections of historical portraits in the world. Don't miss the small castle theatre built by Gustav III (who was also responsible for the Drottningholm Theatre), or the two 16th-century bronze cannon in the outer courtyard, seized in wars with the Russians.

The castle is open May-August daily 10am-4pm, except Whitsun and Midsummer Day. Check with the Stockholm Information Service (see p.123) for times out of season.

Next door to the castle is **Mariefred**, where the steamer to Gripsholm docks. You may want to pause a while in this attractive little town of yellow and red frame houses, with lovely gardens lined up in tight rows beside narrow streets and a cobblestone square. A white baroque church and an 18th-century town hall are two of the highlights.

Before leaving Mariefred you should take a ride on the **Östra Södermanlands Järnväg** (East Södermanland Railway), a rolling museum of vintage coaches pulled by an old steam engine. This narrow gauge railway, which dates from 1895, is maintained by local rail buffs. It runs from Mariefred to Läggesta, a distance of 4km (2½ miles), at a top speed of 11kph (7mph). It's a slow but delightful trip. **61**

NORTH TO UPPSALA

There are three destinations worth visiting on the north shore of Lake Mälaren in the province of Uppland: Sigtuna, Skokloster Castle and Uppsala, linked to the lake by a short canal. All three can be reached easily from Stockholm by train, bus or boat.

The closest to Stockholm is **Sigtuna**, situated on a beautiful, slender arm of the lake. You can drive there in about 45 minutes, or take a train from Centralstationen and change to a bus at Märsta.

Sigtuna, probably Sweden's oldest town, was founded at the beginning of the 11th century by Olof Skötkonung, the country's first Christian king. It served as the religious centre of the country – a role later taken over by Uppsala – and has some of Sweden's oldest churches. It was also Sweden's first capital and a lively trading port, until a series of disasters struck. Estonian pirates raided Sigtuna and burned it to the ground. The town gradually **62** recovered, but Gustav Vasa,

fired by the ideas of the Reformation, shut down its monasteries. The monks left and the town fell into obscurity.

Today Sigtuna is a lakeside idyll with the ruins of four churches, built between 1060 and 1130. Mariakyrkan (St Mary's), which is a monastery church of the 13th-century, remains as mute testimony to Sigtuna's glorious past. Walk along Storgatan, said to be the oldest street in Sweden, and have a look at the quaint, toy-like town hall, dating from 1744. Other points of interest, aside from the church ruins and scattered rune stones from the Viking era, are the Fornhemmet Museum, containing local archaeological finds, and the Lundström House, a good example of late 19th-century architecture and with furniture from the same period.

The Sigtuna Foundation, an important religious institution, recently injected new life into the town. It has played host to many prominent authors and scholars who have come here to put the finishing touches to a book or dissertation in the guest rooms which overlook a cloister and rose garden.

Along this route is **Skokloster**, a magnificent baroque palace on the edge of a lovely bay of Lake Mälaren, about midway between Sigtuna and Uppsala. It was built by Carl Gustaf Wrangel, a field marshal under Gustavus Adolphus in the Thirty Years' War.

The castle's 100 over-sized rooms house a fabulous collection of historical treasures, mostly from the 17th century, when Sweden was Europe's pre-eminent military power.

Here there are silver and glass pieces, tapestries, baroque furniture, over 1,000 paintings and 20,000 rare books and manuscripts, much of it war booty. The arms collection, one of the largest in the world, starts off with crossbows and includes such oddities as a set of executioner's swords and a 2½m (8ft) rifle that belonged to

The old East Södermanland Railway is one of the numerous attractions around Lake Mälaren.

Typical Dalarna red wooden horse, one of the most familiar symbols of Sweden.

Queen Kristina. The castle is open every day and there are guided tours, May-September 11am-4pm.

Skokloster's vast estate also has a restaurant, a modern hotel and a **Motor Museum**, with a fine collection of vintage and veteran cars and engines. The prize exhibits are an 1899 Renault, an elegant maroon 1911 Austin, and a Spitfire engine from the time of the Battle of Britain. The Motor

Museum is open all year round daily 11am-4pm.

History jostles you at virtually every corner in **Uppsala**, an ancient centre of culture, religion and education. It's the seat of the Archbishop of the Swedish Church and home of Uppsala University, one of the world's great institutions of higher learning, which celebrated its 500th anniversary in 1977. The city (with a population of 150,000) lies 73km (46 miles) north of Stockholm and can be reached in an hour by train from Centralstationen.

A quick free-hand sketch of Uppsala would show the river Fyrisån meandering its way through the centre of town, green patina forming on the campus statues, rare and beautiful flowers blooming in the Linnaeus Gardens and the old wooden buildings aging gracefully – in sharp contrast to the new glass and steel structures. Most distinctive of all is Uppsala's skyline silhouette – the twin spires of the cathedral and the round towers of the castle, both centuries-old landmarks, soar over the city.

64

Hotels and Restaurants in Stockholm

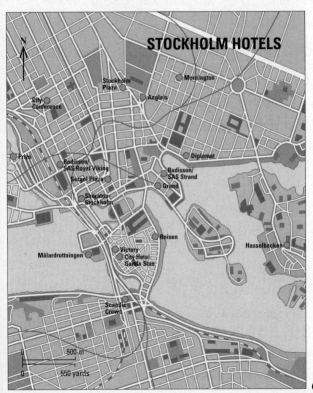

STOCKHOLM HOTELS

N

Mornington

Stockholm Plaza

Anglais

City Conference

Prize

Diplomat

Radisson/ SAS Royal Viking

Sergel Plaza

Radisson/ SAS Strand

Grand

Sheraton-Stockholm

Reisen

Hasselbacken

Mälardrottningen

Victory
City Hotel
Gamla Stan

Scandic Crown

0   500 m

0   550 yards

Recommended Hotels

Hotels are of a consistently high standard, but not cheap. *Moms* (VAT) on hotels is 12%, and there are several hotel packages available. For further information on hotels, see p.100.

The price categories below are based on two people sharing a double room at full rates, including substantial cold-table breakfast, *Moms* and service charge.

▥▥▥	Above 1,800kr
▥▥	1100-1,800kr
▥	Below 1,100kr

STOCKHOLM

Anglais RESO Hotel ▥▥
Humlegårdsgatan 23
S-10220 Stockholm
Tel. 08-614 16 00
Fax 08-611 09 72
Modern hotel opposite Humlegården Park. 212 rooms and a number of comfortable cabins.

City Conference Hotel ▥▥
Wallingatan, S-10724 Stockholm
Tel. 08-20 15 20
Fax 08-791 50 50
Comfortable hotel, quiet and well-planned with an outdoor terrace.

City Hotel Gamla Stan ▥
Lilla Nygatan 25
S-111028 Stockholm
Tel. 08-24 44 50
Fax 08-21 64 83
This hotel occupies a 15th-century building at the Gamla Stan's south end. It is unlicensed, but is popular with the business and budget travellers. 51 rooms.

Claes på Hornet ▥▥
Surbrunnsgatan 20
S-11248 Stockholm
Tel. 08-16 51 30
Fax 08-612 53 15
Once an 18th-century inn, this is now a small hotel (10 rooms only) with a lovely atmosphere. Situated in a quiet area, north of the city centre.

Grand Hotel ▥▥▥
S Blasieholmen 8
S-10383 Stockholm
Tel. 08-679 35 00
Fax 08-611 86 86
Luxury hotel overlooking water to Gamla Stan and the Royal Palace. Old steamers stand in anchorage in the harbour facing it. Excellent restaurants. 321 rooms.

Hasselbacken Hotel

Hazeliusbacken 20
S-10055 Stockholm
Tel. 08-670 50 50
Fax 08-663 84 10
Mansion-style building grafted on to 19th-century timber restaurant. Views over Djurgården Royal Park. Handy for museums, Skansen and Gröna Lund. 112 rooms.

Hotell Diplomat

Strandvägen 7C
S-10440 Stockholm
Tel. 08-663 58 00
Fax 08-783 66 34
Fine waterfront hotel built in 1911 in *Jugendstil*. Looks towards the boats at Nybroviken. From here you can walk to Djurgården Park and Skansen. 133 rooms.

Hotell Mälardrottningen

Riddarholmen
S-11128 Stockholm
Tel. 08-24 36 00
Fax 08-24 36 76
One of Stockholm's most unusual places to stay: boat hotel in 1920s luxury yacht (built 1924) formerly owned by American millionairess Barbara Hutton. Situated in lovely anchorage at Riddarholmen, close to the Old Town. Cabins are now luxury hotel rooms. Gourmet restaurant (see p.72). 59 rooms.

Källhagens Wärdshus

Djurgårdbrunnsvägen 10
S-115267 Stockholm
Tel. 08-667 60 60
Fax 08-667 60 43
Classic modern building (1990) in an idyllic setting 2km (1½ miles) from city centre. It is famous for its food.

Långholmen

Gamla Kronohäktet
S-10072 Stockholm
Tel. 08-668 05 00
Fax 08-84 10 96
Unusual hotel in a former prison. Also offers Youth Hostel accommodation. 101 rooms.

Mornington Hotel

Nybrogatan 53
S-10244 Stockholm
Tel. 08-663 12 40
Fax 08-662 21 79
Central hotel, close to museums. English-style lobby bar and restaurant. 140 rooms.

Prize Hotel

Kungsbron 1
S-11122 Stockholm
Tel. 08-14 94 50
Fax 08-14 98 48
Next door to World Trade Centre building. Breakfast hotel, popular with business travellers, but also a good family hotel. 158 rooms.

67

Radisson/SAS Royal Viking Hotel ▌▌

Vasagatan 1
Box 234, 10124 Stockholm
Tel. 08-14 00 00
Fax 08-10 81 80

Located close to Centralstationen and airport buses. Good restaurants and rooftop bar. 319 rooms.

Radisson/SAS Strand Hotel ▌▌

Nybrokajen 9
Box 16396, S-10327 Stockholm
Tel. 08-678 78 00
Fax 08-611 24 36

Traditional building overlooking boats, with good view from its bar and restaurant on the top floor.

Reisen RESO Hotel ▌▌▌

Skeppsbron 12-14
S-11130 Stockholm
Tel. 08-22 32 60
Fax 08-20 15 59

Well-known 19th-century hotel on waterfront in Gamla Stan. Good sauna. Piano bar. 114 rooms.

Scandic Crown Hotel ▌▌

Guldgrånd 8
Box 15270, S-10465 Stockholm
Tel. 08-702 25 00
Fax 08-642 83 58

Excellent location. Famous restaurant, wine cellar and original spirit shop from 1700. 319 rooms.

Sergel Plaza RESO Hotel ▌▌

Brunkebergstorg 9
Box 16411, S-10327 Stockholm
Tel. 08-22 66 00
Fax 08-21 50 70

On quiet square in centre of Stockholm. Comfortable lobby, café and piano bar, and a good international restaurant. 406 rooms.

Sheraton-Stockholm ▌▌

Tegelbacken 6
Tel. 08-14 26 00
Fax 08-21 70 26

Centrally located, with view of the water and City Hall, as well as first-rate restaurant, lobby bar and popular bistro. 459 rooms.

Stockholm Plaza ▌▌

Birger Jarlsgatan 29
S-10328 Stockholm
Tel. 08-14 51 20
Fax 08-210 34 92

Unusual, stone-built 19th-century hotel with a pleasant atmosphere. 151 rooms.

Victory Hotel ▌▌▌

Lilla Nygatan 5
S-11128 Stockholm
Tel. 08-14 30 90
Fax 08-20 21 77

17th-century building on a quiet street. Famous for its Lord Nelson memorabilia. 48 rooms.

STOCKHOLM ARCHIPELAGO

Grand Hotel Saltsjöbaden

S-13983 Saltsjöbaden
Tel. 08-717 00 20
Fax 08-717 95 31
Castle-style hotel set on the edge of Baggensfjärden. It provides good service and food, and there are swimming, sailing, tennis, fishing and golf facilities available. 105 rooms.

Waxholms Hotell

Hamngatan 2
Box 63, S-18521 Vaxholm
Tel. 08-541 301 50
Fax 08-541 313 76
Comfortable, modest hotel set on Vaxholm island – ideal for watersports. 32 rooms.

LAKE MÄLAREN

Gripsholms Värdshus and Hotel

Kyrkogatan 1
S-64700 Mariefred
Tel. 0159-130 20
Fax 0159-109 74
In close proximity to Mälaren and the boat landing stage, with a good view of Gripsholm Slott. Sauna, gym, billiards and marked walking paths. 45 rooms.

Kohlswa Herrgård

S-73030 Kolsva, near Arboga
Tel. 0221-509 00
Fax 0221-511 80
Surrounded by its own parkland. Riding, fishing, shooting, tennis, golf and walking. 44 rooms.

Sigtunastiftelsens Gästhem

Manfred Björkquists allé 2-4
S-19322 Sigtuna
Tel. 08-592 589 00
Fax 08-592 589 99
Located in woods near Mälaren. Cloister-like building with beautiful rose garden. 51 rooms.

UPPSALA

Hotell Linné

Skolgatan 45
S-75002 Uppsala
Tel. 018-10 20 00
Fax 018-761 74
Excellent location in the heart of Uppsala. Fine restaurant. Closed July. 117 rooms.

Hotell Svava

Bangården 24, Box 1425
S-75144 Uppsala
Tel. 018-13 00 30
Fax 018-13 22 30
Centrally located, close to most sights. Indoor shopping complex. 111 rooms.

69

Recommended Restaurants

Stockholm offers a variety of restaurants. Portions are usually generous and salad is often included. On a tight budget, however, make lunch, *dagens rätt*, the main meal and look out for offers such as Sunday specials. Tourist information publications such as *Stockholm This Week* give listings. Remember that some restaurants may be closed during July.

Eating out in Sweden can be expensive; one reason is that the bill usually includes 21% *Moms* (VAT) and service charge. It is customary to round up the bill to the nearest 10kr.

The establishments listed below offer both quality food and service, and represent good value for money. Prices are for an evening meal per person, without wine.

𝄃𝄃𝄃	above (sometimes well above) 250kr
𝄃𝄃	100-250kr
𝄃	below 100kr

STOCKHOLM

Berns 𝄃𝄃
Nåckströmsgatan 8/Berzelii Park
Tel. 08-614 07 00
One of Europe's biggest restaurants, with a cabaret where international stars like Josephine Baker and Marlene Dietrich once performed. Opulent 19th-century interior with crystal chandeliers and hundreds of gilded fixtures. Good food and great entertainment.

Blå Porten Café 𝄃
Djurgårdsvägen 60
Tel. 08-663 87 59/08-662 71 62
This is an attractive restaurant located in a former art gallery, with a central garden. It serves good, simple food, with the emphasis on Swedish cuisine.

Centralens Restaurang 𝄃𝄃
Centralstationen
Tel. 08-20 20 9
Set directly above the railway station hall, this restaurant offers good food, and is especially popular among travellers for its breakfast. Simple dishes.

Den Gyldene Freden 𝄃𝄃
Österlånggatan 51
Tel. 08-10 90 46
A restaurant and tavern in the Old Town with historic brick cellar rooms. See p.34.

Eriks

Österlånggatan 17
Tel. 08-23 85 00

Erik Lallerstedt, one of Sweden's finest chefs, presides over this restaurant in medieval Gamla Stan. Among many tantalizing fish specialities, including salmon, is grilled crayfish with a garlic-and-parsley flavoured chablis sauce.

Franska Matsalen

Grand Hotel, S Blasieholmen 8
Tel. 08-679 36 84

Very elegant restaurant, with mahogany panelling and crystal chandeliers. Despite the name (French Dining Room), the food is Swedish, prepared with a French touch. Very good wine cellar, and a fine selection of French cheese.

Hasselbacken

Hazeliusbacken 20
Tel. 08-670 50 00

Famous 19th-century restaurant, with the added benefit of a large terrace garden. International and traditional Swedish food served in a beautiful setting.

Hermans, The New Green Kitchen

Stora Nygatan 11
Tel. 08-11 95 00

Highly popular international vegetarian cooking. Its success has spawned a series of other locations throughout the city.

KB

Smålandsgatan 7
Tel. 08-679 60 32

An excellent restaurant and meeting place for successful artists and writers, in the heart of the city. Swedish and French cuisine.

Kajplats 9

Norr Mälarstrand/ Kungsholmstorg
Tel. 08-652 45 45

A waterfront restaurant facing Lake Mälaren, which serves high-quality traditional Swedish fish and shellfish dishes.

Källaren Aurora

Munkbron 11
Tel. 08-21 93 59

An atmospheric cellar restaurant, housed in a fine 17th-century building in Gamla Stan. The speciality is charcoal-grilled *gravad lax* (pickled salmon).

Leijontornet (Victory Hotel)

Lilla Nygatan 5
Tel. 014-23 55

For high-class, traditional Swedish cuisine in historic setting, with a glass floor over the ruins of medieval walls. (Closed July.)

71

Mårtin Trotzig

Västerlånggatan 79
Tel. 08-24 02 31

A new, instantly successful restaurant in an ancient building on Gamla Stan's main walking street. Small menu of first-rate fish and meat dishes.

Mälardrottningen

Riddarholmen
Tel. 08-24 36 00

International and Swedish cuisine is served on what was once Barbara Hutton's luxury yacht.

Opera Bar

Operahuset
Tel. 08-10 79 35

Meeting place for Stockholm's artistic elite ever since it opened in 1904. Splendid art deco interior, with comfortable leather armchairs and marble-topped tables, where you can enjoy a drink and home-cooked Swedish dishes.

Operakällaren

Operahuset
Tel. 08-676 58 00

A venerable institution (dating back some 200 years), with fine décor. Haute cuisine and home cooking. It is especially famous for its wonderful smörgåsbord, and its magnificent wine cellar with some 40,000 bottles.

Stallmästaregården

Nortull
Tel. 08-610 13 01

Located in a garden overlooking a Baltic inlet. It dates back to the 1700s, and the menu is every bit as good as the beautiful location.

Ulriksdals Wärdshus

Solna
Tel. 08-85 08 15

Situated in a royal park in the northern suburb of Solna. First-rate cuisine, with specialities like salmon, snow grouse and reindeer.

Victoria

Kungsträdgården
Tel. 08-10 10 85

Serving good traditional Swedish food and overlooking Stockholm's popular garden square. Open late.

Wedholms Fisk

Nybrokajan 17
Tel. 08-611 78 74

Superb seafood is the speciality here – lobster, sole, perch or pike, fried, grilled or flambée.

Zum Franziskaner

Skeppsbron 44
Tel. 08-411 83 30

Stockholm's oldest restaurant, founded in 1421, with *Jugendstil* décor. It serves Swedish and German home cooking.

Begin your sightseeing at **Uppsala Domkyrka**, right in the middle of the university grounds. This massive 13th-century cathedral with its lofty 122m (400ft) spires took 150 years to complete. Many famous Swedes are buried here: King Gustav Vasa (and his three wives); the remains of St Erik, Sweden's patron saint and king who died a martyr in Uppsala in 1160; Emanuel Swedenborg, mystic, scientist and philosopher; and Carl Linnaeus, the botanist who, like Swedenborg, worked at Uppsala University. In addition to the tombs, the huge interior contains religious tapestries, articles of silver and gold and other objects of great historical and aesthetic interest.

Pause to look at the medieval wall paintings in the **Trinity Church** (*Helga Trefaldighetskyrkan*) nearby before you head off for the

Uppsala Slott (castle), the cathedral's secular rival. This looming red structure, set on a hill overlooking the town, was begun in the 1540s by Gustav Vasa. Having severed ties with the pope, the king intended the castle to be a symbol of royal power. The cannon were therefore aimed directly at the archbishop's residence.

The castle has been the setting of lavish coronation feasts and many dramatic historical

*T*he river Fyrisån provides a calm setting for this view of Uppsala Domkyrka's soaring spires.

events. It was here, for instance, that Gustavus Adolphus held the talks that led Sweden into the Thirty Years' War, and that Queen Kristina gave up her crown in 1654 before setting off for Rome. Today Uppsala Castle serves as the residence of the provincial governor and is used for civic celebrations.

Summer wild flowers embellish the countryside around Uppsala with colour and beauty.

Of the university buildings, the most notable is **Carolina Rediviva**, which now houses the biggest and oldest library in Sweden, founded by Gustavus Adolphus in the 17th century. The collection contains more than two million books and half a million manuscripts and documents, many from medieval times. Among them are extremely rare items, including the **Codex Argenteus** (Gothic Silver Bible), written in the 6th century in silver letters and gold capitals on purple parchment.

You should drop into the **Gustavianum**, a university building topped by a most curious room. This is an octagonal anatomical theatre under a striking dome constructed in 1662 by Olof Rudbeck, one of many brilliant scientists who taught and did research at Uppsala University. He used the room to dissect bodies for medical instruction. The Gustavianum also houses the Victoria Museum of Egyptology collections.

Many people travel to Uppsala with one purpose in mind – to visit places connected with Carl Linnaeus, known throughout the world as the 'Father of Modern Botany' and also the 'Flower King'. Linnaeus came to Uppsala in 1728 as a medical student, was appointed lecturer in botany after only two years at the university, and became a professor of medicine in 1741. In his lifetime Linnaeus named and described some 10,000 different species of plants.

Some of these species can be seen in the university's **Linnéträdgården** (at Svartbäcksgatan 27), which houses 1,300 plants arranged according to species, exactly as they were in Linnaeus' era. His home in the gardens is now a museum which is open to the public.

During the summer months botanists lead groups of visitors on walks along three marked trails, following the footsteps of Linnaeus in the forests around Uppsala. You can also take a guided tour to **Hammarby**, Linnaeus' summer home (13km/8 miles from Uppsala), where he received hundreds of students from all over the world. The garden there is said to contain a number of specimens planted by Linnaeus himself. The Uppsala Tourist Information Centre (which is based in the local Stadshuset) arranges the walks and visits to Hammarby.

Be sure to make the excursion to **Gamla Uppsala** (Old Uppsala), about 3km (2 miles) out of town, reached by regular bus service from the city centre. This is the site of the ruins of a pagan temple and three huge burial mounds said to contain the remains of kings **75**

This strikingly eccentric parish church has towered over a former pagan site since medieval times.

mentioned in the epic *Beowulf*. The graves, dating from the 6th century, are called Kungshögarna (Kings' Hills).

A medieval parish church stands solidly on the remnants of the heathen temple where blood flowed profusely when human and animal sacrifices were offered up to the gods. Close by is Disagården, an impressive open-air museum, and the Odinsburg Inn, where you can drink mead (*mjöd*) from old Viking ox-horns.

While Uppsala is a tranquil place most of the year, there is one special occasion when suppressed emotions virtually explode. This takes place on Walpurgis Night, in tradition a half-pagan, half-Christian celebration, which is held on the last day of April. The ceremony begins in the afternoon, when the undergraduates and friends gather in front of the Carolina Rediviva and, at a signal from the rector of the university, the students let out a huge cheer before donning their white student caps. The celebration goes on into the evening, when the whole university – students, professors and alumni – march with flaming torches and flags of the 'nations' (that is, student clubs representing different Swedish provinces) to the summit of the castle hill. Here they burst into songs hailing the country and the arrival of spring. The festivities continue at the student clubs until the early hours of the morning.

What to Do

Shopping

Shopping in Stockholm is a delightful experience, an entry into a very special world of design. The best-known products are those of the industrial arts and handicrafts, such as glassware, ceramics, stainless-steel cutlery, silver, furniture and textiles. Sweden's fine reputation in these fields rests on an old tradition of skilled craftsmanship passed down through the generations. Contemporary Swedish design has its roots in the peasant art of the past.

You'll find a broad range of shops and department stores in Stockholm – many of which are themselves very beautiful. English is widely spoken.

Most Stockholm shops open from 9am to 6pm on weekdays, but close early on Saturday, some time between 1pm and 4pm. During the winter, department stores stay open later on certain days and may also open on Sundays.

Value-Added Tax Refunds

VAT, or sales tax, called *Moms* in Sweden, is 25 per cent on all products (and on most services). However, there is a Tax-Free Shopping Scheme in operation, whereby *Moms* will be refunded in cash at any point of departure to visitors who buy in shops displaying the blue-and-yellow 'Tax-Free Shopping' sticker. You need to present your passport at the shop. Later, you simply hand over the Tax-Free Shopping Cheque provided by the shop (be sure to fill out the back) at the Tax-Free Service counter in ports, airports and on ships. Note that refunds apply for a limited period after purchase, and are available to non-Scandinavian residents only.

Where to Shop

There are three large department stores in the centre. One is PUB, on the corner of Drottninggatan and Kungsgatan, a half block from Hötorget. The open-air market at Hötorget makes this as good a place as any to start a shopping tour.

From PUB work your way south along Drottninggatan to Åhléns department store and Sergels Torg. An underground shopping mall then brings you directly to the basement of NK, Stockholm's classic department store. Head east from

*F*ew shops in Stockholm are as popular with shoppers as the up-market NK department store.

NK along Hamngatan until you come to Norrmalmstorg. Turn left into Biblioteksgatan, a short, car-free street which will take you to Stureplan. Then head west along broad Kungsgatan and you'll soon be back to the starting point.

For fun shopping in a marvellous medieval milieu, try exploring Gamla Stan. Västerlånggatan, the pedestrian street bisecting the island, is lined with shops and restaurants. You'll find smaller shops and boutiques among the lanes that branch off Västerlånggatan.

The gift shop in the Royal Palace is worth visiting for its array of unusual souvenirs.

Stockholm's main markets are the colourful Östermalmstorg, an indoor market noted for its cheese and fish specialities, and Hötorget, a lively outdoor market where the locals buy their food from Monday to Saturday and shop for crafts on Sunday. What is reputedly the largest flea market in Scandinavia takes place at weekends in Skärholmen Center, a 20-minute ride by *tunnelbana* from central Stockholm.

Good Buys

Glassware. This is Sweden's most famous design product – and one of your best buys. Names such as Orrefors, Kosta and Boda are well-known all over the world, and the talented artists and artisans working for these and other glassworks ensure that their reputation for creative design and high quality will live on.

Swedish glassware is expensive; however, some glassworks sell items for less than you would pay in a shop.

Ceramics. Rörstrand and Gustavsberg are the predominant names in this field, but there are many smaller companies. Here again, there is a wide choice, ranging from charming and fanciful items that easily fit your suitcase and wallet to one-of-a-kind sculptures with a price tag to match their considerable size.

Once again, if you are visiting a ceramic factory, you may find something suitable that is priced below what you would have to pay in a shop.

Home Furnishings. Swedes have a deep – almost fanatical – fondness for the home and its furnishings, and this is reflected in the tremendous care that goes into the production of furniture. The modern classics of masters like Bruno Mathsson and Carl Malmsten are largely responsible for the numerous plaudits Sweden has gained in this field, but the tradition of good-looking, functional furniture is carried on by the younger craftsmen.

Stainless Tableware. This is another superb national product that has won international recognition. Swedish cutlery, **79**

or flatware, is not only beautiful, but makes a fine gift to take home.

Souvenirs. Brightly painted, hand-carved Dala horses are very probably the most typical Swedish souvenirs and certainly the most popular. These wooden red horses are named after the province of Dalarna, where they originated. More than anything else they represent the traditions and folklore of the region, and perhaps the country. Among other items worth buying are the painted linen tapestries and the lovely handmade dolls.

Lapp Handicrafts. Although Stockholm is far from Lappland (which extends beyond the Arctic Circle), many shops sell a range of buckles, knife handles, pouches and other handcrafted Lapp items that have been skilfully made from reindeer antlers and skin.

Suede. Coats, jackets and even skirts made out of suede are excellent buys in Stockholm. Suede, in fact, is a Swedish

Swedish craftsmen are reputed for quality work, such as these wooden puzzles for children.

invention, and also the French word for Sweden.

Silver. Silversmiths like Sigurd Persson continue to turn out bold, innovative necklaces, bracelets and rings. They also fashion stunning silver bowls, cigarette cases and the like.

Clogs. These Swedish wooden shoes, called *träskor*, have become popular in many parts of the world. They are available in Stockholm's shops in a wide range of models.

Cameras. These are a particularly good buy in Sweden, and include Hasselblad, the Swedish camera used in space by American astronauts.

Sporting Goods. The Swedes, being such keen campers, are renowned for their excellent camping equipment, as well as the fishing rods and reels made by ABU, a Swedish company that has become one of the world's biggest exporters of high-quality fishing gear.

Candles. Swedes create a cosy mood during the long winter nights by using candles to light their homes. You'll find them sold in all imaginable sizes, shapes and colours. The variety of candlesticks – in all kinds of materials from glass and metal to wood and straw – is equally broad.

Christmas Decorations. For Swedes Christmas is a time of strong tradition, and the yuletide ornaments are frequently very attractive. Larger department stores, having realized the decorations' potential as souvenirs, are today offering tourists a small selection of these splendid holiday items all year round.

Food. Just before you leave Stockholm, don't forget to buy a selection of Swedish cheese, herring, caviar, smoked salmon, crisp bread and – last but not least – a bottle of aquavit, the popular national drink, so that you can entertain your friends back home with a little *smörgåsbord*.

Entertainment

No one would claim that the entertainment possibilities in Stockholm are equal to those of, say, New York or London. However, enough goes on in this town to satisfy the desires of any visitor. Moreover, the long, light Stockholm summer nights are made to order for pleasurable outdoor activities.

An indispensable guide to what's happening in the city is *Stockholm This Week*, which is published by the Stockholm Information Service. It's available free at your hotel.

Music and Theatre

The massive auditorium of the Stockholm Konserthuset is the main venue for serious music during the winter months, the season stretching from September to May or June. In summer you can enjoy **concerts** in the many splendid settings scattered throughout the Stockholm area – in the Royal Palace, in the courtyard of the Hallwylska Museet, at Prince Eugen's Waldemarsudde, in St Jacob's Church and the German Church in the Old Town. There are also open-air concerts in many of the city parks, including Kungsträdgården in the heart of town.

The refined sounds of a classical musician busking for a living is one of Stockholm's charms.

First-rate **opera** and **ballet** are offered at Operan (Royal Opera) from early autumn to late spring. In summer the Drottningholm Court Theatre (see p.59) stages 17th- and 18th-century drama. And you should check to see if the Cullberg Ballet Company, formed by the choreographer Birgit Cullberg, is performing during your stay in Stockholm.

Modern and classical **plays** are staged at Kungliga Dramatiska Teatern and Stadsteatern (Stockholm Municipal Theatre) – in Swedish only. And the Marionette Theatre puts on puppet and marionette productions for children and adults.

There are many **cinemas** in the city centre, and all foreign films are shown in their original language but with Swedish subtitles. Check the evening newspapers to see what's on.

Top spots for **jazz** are the Stampen, a pub in the Old Town, and Fasching Jazzclub at Kungsgatan. The Stockholm Jazz and Blues Festival is held during the last weekend in June and the first weekend in July on Skeppsholmen.

Nightlife

Night owls will be pleased that the sidewalks in Stockholm are no longer rolled up at midnight. Many of the **nightclubs**, including a few at hotels, now stay open until 3am and later. All have live dance music; some also offer cabaret and variety shows. If you sit at a table you are expected to eat, but at the bar ordering food is unnecessary. There are also **dance restaurants** in town that close earlier, at around 1am. Unattached males and unescorted females tend to be the rule at Stockholm dance restaurants and nightclubs, so these are good places to meet people.

Parks

The famous open-air museum of **Skansen** (see p.39) has a full and varied summer season of outdoor entertainment. This may include anything from a performance by an orchestra to a foreign dance troupe.

Another focal point of enjoyable summer entertainment is Skansen's close neighbour, **83**

Sports

The Swedes are a very sports-minded people, so it's not surprising that excellent sporting facilities exist throughout the Stockholm region. Top spectator sports are soccer in the summer and ice hockey in the winter. The prestigious sports events, such as the ice hockey championships, are held in the Globe Arena, whose gigantic white dome you may have noticed on the city's south horizon. Reputed to be the largest spherical building anywhere in the world, the Arena can be transformed rapidly from a sports stadium into a theatre or a concert hall.

Watersports such as sailing, swimming and fishing are very popular, as you would expect in a city that virtually floats on water. Swedes of all ages are also fond of jogging and cross-country skiing, and there are many such trails in nearby wooded areas.

A number of recreational facilities are centred in Djurgården, where you can hire a bike, go horseback riding and enjoy

I n a city so steeped in water it is hardly surprising that Stockholmers are keen on sailing.

Tivoli Gröna Lund, on the shore of Djurgården. Crowds flock to the amusement park's open-air stage to be entertained by international performers, which have included in the past such diverse figures as Count Basie and Sven-Bertil Taube. The amusements are open to the public from late April to early September, **84** until 10pm in midsummer.

peaceful promenading. Get in touch with the Stockholm Information Service (see p.123) for up-to-date information on sports around the city.

Swimming. In the Stockholm region there are about 200km (125 miles) of beaches – both sea and lake bathing – including several at Riddarfjärden near the centre of town. Bear in mind that the water hardly ever gets really warm (above 20°C/68°F). If this is too cold for you, there are seven outdoor pools in the city, some with saunas, and dozens of others in the suburbs, open from May to mid-September. One of the most pleasant pools is Vanadisbadet, near Sveavägen, which has been converted into a beautiful water park with water slides. The biggest is Eriksdalsbadet, on the south side of the city, which can accommodate 3,000 people. Nude bathing is not allowed.

Fishing. Pollution has been eliminated from Stockholm's waters in the last few years, and it's now possible to fish for salmon in Strömmen, the stream that flows past the Royal Palace. There is good fishing in Lake Mälaren, the smaller lakes in the city environs and around the 24,000 islands of the archipelago in the Baltic Sea. A fishing permit is required, but fairly easy to obtain. You can get them from local tourist offices, certain hotels and some shops and petrol stations. For more information call the Swedish Sport Angling and Fishery Conservation Association in Stockholm; tel. 08-795 33 50.

Sailing. For sailing enthusiasts there is plenty of company in Stockholm. During the summer months there are almost as many boats as cars – in Lake Mälaren, in the Baltic and skimming through the city's waterways. There are at least 10 different places in the Stockholm area where boats can be rented (again, check with the tourist office) and special harbours for visitors with their own boats. But a word of warning: if you are planning to sail through the **85**

labyrinth of islands that make up the Stockholm archipelago, you need to know what you're doing. It's a beautiful experience, but not to be attempted by amateurs.

Canoeing. Sweden is very well equipped for canoeists. For information contact Svenska Kanotförbundet, Idrottens Hus, Storforsplan 44, 123 87 Farsta; tel. 08-605 60 00.

Stockholm Water Festival

The annual Stockholm Water Festival, launched in 1990, has been a success well beyond the wildest dreams of its organizers. It quickly became Europe's biggest fun fair, drawing more than four million visitors.

For 10 days every August, downtown Stockholm – where the waters of Lake Mälaren and the Baltic meet – is cordoned off to create a space for some 1,500 different events to take place. These include plays, opera and musicals performed on open-air stages, as well as pageants, circus acts, concerts by symphony and rock orchestras, and dance recitals.

Other festival features are flea markets, jousting tournaments near the Royal Palace and waterskiing races on Lake Mälaren. Food and drink, including vast amounts of crayfish and beer, are provided by restaurants and dozens of street stalls.

An international fireworks competition is the high point. Various countries, which in the past have included Spain, Germany, France, Italy, Australia and the United States, take part in the extravaganza that lights up the city centre sky and water.

During the festival the Stockholm Water Prize, of more than one million kronor, is presented by King Carl XVI Gustaf at a formal dinner in the City Hall. It's awarded to the person, anywhere in the world, deemed to have done the most significant work in water pollution, purification and conservation.

Golf. There are now about 200 courses in Sweden, including one beyond the Arctic Circle, where it's possible to play under the light of the midnight sun. In the Stockholm area the following 27-hole golf courses stand out: Djursholms Golfklubb, Ågesta Golfklubb, Lindö Golfklubb and Saltsjöbadens Golfklubb.

Tennis. You might have some trouble getting a court in the evening and at the weekend, but otherwise it should be all right. Two of the very best venues, which have indoor and outdoor courts, are Tennisstadion Fiskartorpsvägen 20 and the Kungliga Tennishallen, Lidingövägen 75.

Hiking. The hallowed tradition of *allemansrätten* guarantees everyone an equal right to enjoy nature. This means that you can walk just about anywhere you want in Sweden, as long as you don't damage anyone else's property. There are plenty of easy waymarked walking trails. The summer trails are indicated by raised or

Getting colour in your hair is in the spirit of the Water Festival fun extravaganza.

painted stones and all-season ones by crosses. For those in search of the more organized itineraries, marked trails start just outside Stockholm. Ambitious hikers can follow a trail called 'Upplandsleden', from Järfälla to Uppsala and from Bålsta to Enköping. To the east of Stockholm, the trail called 'Roslagsleden' extends 56km (35 miles) between Danderyd and Domarudden. **87**

If on a mountain hike that will take more than a day to return to base, you should find out about STF (Svenska Turistföreningen) mountain huts that provide nightly shelter, located at 20km intervals along routes. For more information, obtain the hiking guide *Låglandsleder* from STF, at Drottninggatan 31, Stockholm.

Skating. The most popular and most conspicuous outdoor rink is in Kungsträdgaården in the centre of town. However, many Swedes do prefer long-distance skating along the frozen waterways of Lake Mälaren and the Baltic Sea in winter, when the ice is thick enough. You can hire skates.

Skiing. Swedes enjoy skiing, both the downhill and cross-country versions. There are several ski resorts in Stockholm and at Västmanland, north of Lake Mälaren. A particularly fine ski centre is at Mora on Lake Siljan. For cross-country skiing you will need a map of the route and suitable clothing.

Children

Children can have a lot of fun in Stockholm, a city with a large number of family activities that appeals to both young and old. One major attraction not to be overlooked is the archipelago with its countless islets. Many children ask for nothing better than a boat ride and the chance to climb among the rocks, or to fish or swim. However, there are numerous other highlights in the city to keep children well occupied.

On all public transport in Stockholm, children under 7 years of age travel free, while children between 7 and 18 pay half price. With a Stockholm Card, which enables free travel on the underground, buses and local trains, two children under 18 may be included when accompanied by an adult who has purchased the card (see p.118).

Skansen: this open-air museum's zoo has a section devoted to baby farm animals that children can get close to and pet. And there is an aquarium and a crocodile pond.

Calendar of Events

The Swedes may be ultra-modern in their social and sexual attitudes, but they are very traditional when it comes to celebrations. Throughout the year, festivals brighten up the calendar. (For a comprehensive list of public holidays in Sweden, see p.121.)

30 April: Walpurgis Night has its roots in Viking times. Huge bonfires blaze across the landscape to salute the arrival of spring. The university towns are especially exuberant. Students hold torchlight parades and toast spring in verse, speeches and song.

1 May: May Day is given over to labour groups.

June: on Archipelago Boat Day numerous steam boats make their way over to Vaxholm Island.

6 June: the Swedish National Day is celebrated with flags, parades and supersonic jets streaking across the sky. There is a ceremony when the King and Royal Family (Queen Silvia in Swedish national costume) present flags to organizations and individuals.

Friday between June 19 and 25: on the longest day of the year (Midsummer Eve) colourful maypoles decorated with garlands of birch boughs and wildflowers are raised in village and town squares all over Sweden. After the maypole goes up, everyone joins hands and dances around it to the tunes of country fiddlers. The dancing, along with a fair amount of drinking and merry-making, continues far into the night, which in midsummer is as bright as day. In Stockholm, anyone can join the festivities at Skansen.

August: the Stockholm Water Festival is nowadays the biggest fun fair in Europe (see p.86).

October: the world's largest cross-country race is held at Lidingö.

December: Nobel Prize Day takes place on 10 December.

13 December: one of the winter highlights is St Lucia Day, a beguiling pre-Christmas ceremony. Young girls dressed in long white gowns are crowned with wreaths of lighted candles that symbolize light breaking into the winter darkness. They sing a special Lucia song and serve fresh buns and coffee. If you're in Sweden on this day, you'll see candles in almost every coffee shop and restaurant. **89**

Tekniskamuseet (Technical Museum): older children will be fascinated by the exhibits, especially by the computers.

Aquaria: at this fascinating water museum in Djurgården, among other attractions children can follow the course of a rainforest river from the mountains to the open sea.

*P*ony rides are only one of the many delights that children can indulge in at Skansen.

Hobby & Leksaksmuseet: a variety of toys are on display in the Hobby & Toy Museum.

Gröna Lund: this amusement park, which is only open during the summer months, has rides, a Fun House, and other amusing activities for children. You can buy a daily pass bracelet or coupons for a set number of attractions.

Restaurants: many restaurants have special children's menus, often at half price. In Stockholm there are also many popular fastfood chains.

Eating Out

'Natural' is the best way to describe the Swedish approach to food. A Swede can become quite lyrical at the thought of *färskpotatis*, a dish of new potatoes boiled with dill (a commonly used herb in Sweden) and served with a pat of butter. Wild berries and mushrooms are highly prized, especially since food prices have skyrocketed in recent years.

Swedish law gives everyone the right, known as *allemansrätten*, to wander through fields and forests to pick these gifts of nature. Even the city-dwellers, who are never too far away from the great outdoors, take the opportunity to gather *smultron* (wild strawberries), *blåbär* (bilberries, or blueberries), *hjortron* (Arctic cloudberries), *svamp* (mushrooms) and *lingon* (wild cranberries).

In Sweden each season has its traditional specialities, and any discussion of eating habits has to take these into account. Some regional dishes, such as blood soup and fermented herring, may sound less than appetizing, but those tourists with more adventurous palates will want to try at least a few of those things that the calendar and time-honoured custom prescribe.

Restaurants

Stockholm offers a great variety of dining establishments. During recent years, pizzerias, hamburger chains and Chinese restaurants have spread like wildfire. Others specialize in the food of France, Germany, Spain, Hungary and Greece. The real problem nowadays is finding genuine, old-fashioned Swedish food.

Look out for restaurants that serve *husmanskost* – which are traditional everyday Swedish dishes. These are some you might try: *Janssons frestelse* (Jansson's Temptation), a delicious casserole of potatoes, sprats, onion and cream; *Kåldolmar*, stuffed cabbage rolls; *pytt i panna*, finely cut meat, onions and potatoes; *kalops*, beef stew; *dillkött*, lamb or veal in dill sauce; *köttbullar*, **91** the famous Swedish meatballs; *bruna bönor*, which are baked brown beans in a molasses sauce; *strömmingsflundror*, a fried boned herring; and on Thursday, join almost the entire local populace in eating *ärter med fläsk*, yellow pea soup with pork, followed by *pannkakor med sylt*, pancakes with jam.

The *smörgåsbord* can sometimes be hard to find – except on Sunday afternoons and also during the Christmas season.

*D*ining aboard an old-style paddle-steamer is a good way to relax at the end of a busy day.

Every day the elegant Operakällaren (the Opera Restaurant) in Stockholm has a luncheon *smörgåsbord*, which is reputed to be the best in the world. Otherwise, ask the receptionist at your hotel for advice on this subject.

Eating out in Stockholm is not exactly cheap, but prices at the top-flight restaurants are generally in line with comparable establishments in other European cities. Having predinner cocktails in a restaurant or bar, on the other hand, can make a real dent in your budget. The best thing is to have wine or beer with your meal.

There are many inexpensive self-service cafeterias throughout the city, and most restaurants have small portions for children at half price. Also look for the *Dagens rätt* (dish of the day), as this is usually a good bet.

Lunch tends to be served around noon, and dinner from 6pm. A 13 per cent service charge is normally added to the restaurant bill, though the waiter or waitress may also hope for a small extra tip.

Breakfast and Bread

A Swedish breakfast (*frukost*) usually consists of a cup of coffee or tea with rolls, butter and marmalade and sometimes cheese. If you wake up feeling peckish, a much more substantial breakfast with eggs, bacon or ham will certainly be available at your hotel.

Coffee – which is excellent in Sweden – is consumed in great quantities at all times of the day and night and forms a recognized part of Swedish social life. The Swedes (even adults) also drink a lot of milk with their meals. In addition, yoghurt and other kinds of fermented milk are popular.

Until recently, many people complained about the Swedish bread (which has molasses in it) as being too sweet. As a result, unsweetened bread is being made and widely sold. Be sure to try *knäckebröd* (crisp rye bread), which comes in a wide assortment. This is something worth taking back home along with some cheese – there are, so it is claimed, more than 200 different kinds

to choose from. Look for *vasterbottenost*, *herrgardsost* and *sveciaost* – these are typical hard, well-aged cheeses.

Spring and Summer Specialities

As the name implies, *fettisdagsbullar* or *semlor* (Shrove Tuesday buns) are associated with Lent, but they are now so popular that they appear on the market right after Christmas. The baked buns are split, filled with an almond paste and whipped cream, and then they are served in a deep dish with hot milk, sugar and cinnamon. The arrival of spring is traditionally celebrated with another calory-packed treat, *våfflor* (crisp waffles served with jam and whipped cream), as well as three salmon delicacies – *gravad lax*, pickled salmon in dill served with mustard sauce, *färskrökt lax*, smoked salmon, and *kokt lax*, boiled salmon.

Summertime means almost 24-hour daylight in Sweden. It's a season when people in this northern clime can luxuriate in fruit and vegetables that **93** have been grown locally under the midnight sun, instead of the expensive imported produce available during much of the year. Look for *västkustsallad*, a delicious seafood salad that also contains tomatoes and mushrooms.

A delightful custom not to be missed by anyone visiting

T his Gamla Stan (Old City) café serves lavish amounts of fabulous ice-cream.

Sweden in August is the *kräftor* (crayfish) party. This is when Swedes abandon all rules of table etiquette as they attack mounds of small lobster-like creatures gleaming bright red in the light from gay paper lanterns strung above the tables. *Kryddost*, cheese spiced with caraway, and buttered toast and fresh berries complete the traditional menu. The mood can become quite festive as liberal amounts of aquavit are usually downed on this occasion.

This highly potent drink accompanies another seasonal speciality, *surströmming* (salted and fermented Baltic herring). Indeed, many people can't get this fish past their nose without the aid of a dram or two of aquavit. The smell, to put it mildly, is staggering. Even so, some Swedes, particularly those from the northern part of the country, consider it a great delicacy.

Autumn and Winter Fare

Although southern Sweden is the best place to celebrate St Martin's Day, you can usually find restaurants in Stockholm that observe the tradition as well. The star of this November event is *stekt gås* (roast goose), but the first course and dessert probably deserve the most attention. You begin the meal with a highly spiced *svartsoppa* (blood soup) and finish with *spettekaka*, a lace-like pyramid cake baked on a spit. It melts in your mouth.

The Christmas season gets off to an early, charming start in Sweden on 13 December – one of the darkest and shortest days of the year – when Lucia makes her early morning appearance in many homes and even in public places. Dressed in a long white robe, and with a crown of lighted candles on her head, the Queen of Light awakens the sleeping house by singing the special Lucia song and serving saffron buns, ginger snaps and coffee.

Christmas is preceded by weeks of preparation in the kitchen. Though no longer the feast it once was, the Yuletide *smörgåsbord (julbord)* still retains its essential ingredients. Restaurants also often make a special feature of the *smörgåsbord* at Christmas time.

However, the *smörgåsbord* is only part of the Swedish holiday menu. Other dishes are *lutfisk* (cod that has been dried and cured in lye), *risgrynsgröt* (rice porridge that contains one almond destined for the person to be wed in the coming year) and some *skinka* (ham). This time of year also brings forth all kinds of delicious breads and pastries. **95**

The Smörgåsbord

Bounded by the sea and with some 96,000 lakes dotting its countryside, Sweden has an abundant supply of fish, which naturally plays an important role in the country's diet. In the old days fish was often dried, smoked, cured or fermented to preserve it for the winter. Even today, in the age of the deep-freeze, these methods are still among some of the favourite ways of preparing herring and other treasures from the sea. The herring buffet, or *sillbord*, the predecessor of the *smörgåsbord*, is still the basis of Sweden's most famous culinary attraction.

The *smörgåsbord* table (or groaning board, if you will) can consist of as many as 100 different dishes. It should not be tackled haphazardly. The first thing to remember is not to overload your plate – you can go back to the table as many times as you wish.

Even more important is the order in which you eat. Start off by sampling the innumerable herring dishes, taken with boiled potatoes and bread and butter. Then you move on to other seafood, like smoked or boiled salmon, smoked eel, Swedish caviar and shrimps. Next come the delightful egg dishes, cold meats (try the smoked reindeer) and salads. The small warm dishes eventually loom on the horizon – meat balls, fried sausages and

A Stockholm restaurant displays the dishes in a typical Swedish smörgåsbord.

omelets – and finally (if you still have room), you end up with cheese and fruit.

Alcoholic Beverages

The Swedish national drink is aquavit, also called *snaps*, distilled from potatoes or grain and flavoured with herbs and spices. There are many varieties. Aquavit should always be consumed with food, especially herring; it should be ice-cold and served up in small glasses, consumed straight in a grand gulp or two and washed down with a beer or mineral water. It is closely linked to the word *skål*, that universally recognized Scandinavian toast, delivered as you look straight into the eyes of your drinking companion.

Among other Swedish alcoholic specialities are *glögg*, a hot, spiced wine that appears during the Christmas season, and *punsch* (punch), which is usually served after dinner, well chilled, with coffee. It can also be drunk hot with the traditional Thursday dinner of yellow pea soup and pancakes.

Teetotaller organizations are a powerful factor in Swedish politics and this has led to very high taxes on alcoholic beverages, especially hard liquor, as a means of trying to discourage drinking. Also, with the exception of a very weak beer that can be bought in grocery stores or supermarkets, alcoholic beverages are sold only in the shops of the Systembolaget, the state-owned liquor monopoly.

These Systembolaget shops do stock a vast range of recognized brands of whisky, vodka, gin and so forth, but wine is by far the best value for money. Popular table wines (which are French, Italian, Spanish and Greek) are shipped to Sweden in huge tankers and bottled here. The quality is good, the selection is wide and the prices are relatively moderate. This is all part of the Systembolaget campaign which involves promoting the drinking of wine (but in moderate quantities, of course) while at the same time conducting a propaganda campaign against the evils of consuming hard liquor.

97

To Help You Order ...

Could we have a table?	**Finns det något ledigt bord?**
Do you have a set menu?	**Har ni någon meny?**
I'd like a/an/some ...	**Jag skulle vilja ha ...**
beer	**öl**
bread	**bröd**
butter	**smör**
cheese	**ost**
coffee	**kaffe**
cream	**grädde**
dessert	**efterrätt**
fish	**fisk**
fruit	**frukt**
ice-cream	**glass**

meat	**kött**
menu	**matsedeln**
milk	**mjölk**
mineral water	**mineralvatten**
potatoes	**potatis**
sandwich	**smörgås**
soup	**soppa**
sugar	**socker**
tea	**te**
wine	**vin**

... and Read the Menu

biff	beef steak
böckling	smoked herring
fläskkotlett	pork chop
fromage	mousse
gädda	pike
jordgubbar	strawberries
kalv	veal
kasseler	smoked pork loin
korv	sausage
krabba	crab
krusbär	gooseberries
kyckling	chicken
lammstek	roast lamb
lax	salmon
lever	liver
lök	onion

matjessill	pickled herring
musslor	mussels, clams
nyponsoppa	rose hip soup
oxstek	roast beef
paj	pie
räkor	shrimps
rensadel	saddle of reindeer
rödspätta	plaice
rotmos	mashed turnips
sillbullar	herring rissoles
skaldjur	shellfish
skinka	ham
sparris	asparagus
spenat	spinach
vitkål	white cabbage

BLUEPRINT
for a
Perfect Trip

An A–Z Summary of Practical Information and Facts

Listed after many entries is an appropriate Swedish translation, usually in the singular, plus a number of phrases you may find useful during your stay.

A

ACCOMMODATION (*hotell; logi*)
(See also CAMPING on p.103, YOUTH HOSTELS on p.131 and the list of RECOMMENDED HOTELS starting on p.65)

Hotels in Stockholm, as elsewhere in Sweden, have a well-deserved reputation for cleanliness and good service, regardless of their price category. You would be well advised to book accommodation in advance. Before leaving home, get a copy of the excellent annual brochure published by the Swedish Travel and Tourism Council, entitled *Hotels in Sweden*, which has details about amenities and prices. Ask for it at the Swedish tourist office in your country (see TOURIST INFORMATION OFFICES on p.123) or at your travel agency.

At the same time, enquire about the Stockholm Package, an option that includes hotel, breakfast and the Stockholm Card (see p.118). Also worth looking into is the Hotel Cheque system, enabling you to get cut-rate prices at some 250 Swedish hotels. This is especially useful if you plan to see some of the country outside of Stockholm. You can book your first night in Sweden before you leave home, then make reservations (free) for the following nights through the reception desk of each hotel. Children up to 12 can stay free if they share the parents' room. The Hotel Cheques are valid between mid-June and 1 September. Note that many hotels offer special terms during the summer months and at weekends all year round.

Hostels. Youth hostels in Sweden are open to everyone, irrespective of age. Many have special rooms suitable for motorists with children under 16, and may be worth considering when travelling outside Stockholm. (See YOUTH HOSTELS on p.131)

Hotel Reservation Service. Should you arrive in Stockholm without having booked accommodation, get in touch with Hotellcentralen, run by the tourist office, to find a room in a hotel, boarding house or youth hostel. There is a reservation bureau in the Arlanda airport and at the Central Railway Station. They can be contacted by telephone on 08-24 08 80. During high season they are open daily until late at night; in low season they are open during regular weekday hours.

Do you have any vacancies?	**Har ni några lediga rum?**
I'd like a single/double room.	**Jag skulle vilja ha ett enkelrum/dubbelrum.**
with bath/shower/private toilet	**med bad/dusch/toalett på rummet**
How much does it cost per night/week?	**Vad kostar det per natt/vecka?**

AIRPORTS (flygplats)

All flights to Stockholm are handled by Arlanda airport, located 38km (24 miles) from the city. The airport has four terminals – three for domestic flights and one for international flights. There are inter-terminal buses to transfer passengers between the terminals. The airport telephone number is 08-797 60 00.

Arlanda's international terminal has a first-class restaurant, self-service buffet, bar, Swedish food shop, gift boutiques, duty-free shop, news-stands and book-stands as well as a post office, bank and nursery. There are also car hire desks and tourist information booths where you can book accommodation.

Although taxis are plentiful they are expensive, and for a fraction of the fare you can take an airport bus into town (which takes about 40 minutes). These buses make three stops: near a motor hotel at Ulriksdals Trafikplats on the northern outskirts of the city; St Eriksplan; and Cityterminalen, near the railway station in the city centre. SAS do offer a limousine service to any address in the surrounding area, but it is expensive, though less so if you share the trip.

Domestic flights. Domestic routes are served by Linjeflyg and SAS, and operate from the Arlanda domestic terminals, linked to the international terminal by a 300m (328 yards) walkway and by buses.

Where are the luggage trolleys (carts)?	**Var finns bagagekärrorna?**
Where's the bus into town?	**Var är buss till stan?**

BICYCLE HIRE/RENTAL (*cykel*)

Sweden's roads tend to be uncluttered, so cycling is a popular pastime and bicycles can be hired almost anywhere. The tourist office will provide a list of local operators. You can hire a bicycle at Skepp och Hoch, a rental shop near Djurgårdsbron (the bridge leading to Djurgården). Note that heavy traffic can make bicycling in Stockholm difficult – except in a few places like Djurgården, the big island park. The typical cost of hiring a bicycle is 80kr for a day and 300-400kr for a week.

Outside the city, especially in the island provinces like Öland and Gotland, which are ideally suited to cycling, local tourist offices offer package deals that include accommodation and itineraries planned for you. Get in touch with Svenska Turistföreningen (Swedish Touring Club), which has around 30 such package itineraries of varying length, at: STF, Box 25, Drottninggatan 31-33, 10120 Stockholm; tel. 08-790 31 00.

CAMPING

Sweden has more than 500 camping sites that are officially approved and rated by one, two or three stars according to the facilities offered. Many camping sites are by a lake or the sea, with boats, canoes and bikes for hire, and in some cases horse-riding, mini-golf and tennis facilities. Most are open June-August; however, some are open earlier, though not with their full range of facilities.

In the vicinity of Stockholm are Bredäng Camping (approximately 15 minutes' drive north of the centre of town), Rösjön in Sollentuna, and Ängby Camping in the suburb of Bromma. For a complete list of sites get a copy of *Campingboken* (The Camping Book) published by Svenska Campingvärdars Riksförbund, available at any Swedish bookshop.

If you don't have an International Camping Card you can get a Swedish card issued by Sveriges Campingvärdars Riksförbund (SCR) for only a few kronor at campsites in Sweden, along with a free camping guide. Camping cheques are valid in most sites and allow you to stay at reduced rates. Upon purchase, you get complete information on different sites and surrounding areas.

According to the tradition of *allemansrätten* (Everyone's Right; see p.86), visitors may camp for one night on any private property without the owner's permission (not with caravan), but there are exceptions, so it's always best to ask. Make sure that tents are not pitched too close to dwellings or gardens and that the grounds are left undamaged and unlittered.

Cabins. These are available for rent (with beds and sleeping for 2-6 people) at very reasonable rates. You use your own sleeping bag but kitchen facilities are usually provided. Ask for a list at any campsite in Sweden.

Is there a campsite near here?   **Finns det någon campingplats i närgeten?**

CAR HIRE/RENTAL (biluthyrning)
(See also DRIVING IN SWEDEN on p.108 and PLANNING YOUR BUDGET on p.118)

All of the major international car hire agencies (Avis, Hertz, Budget, Europcar) are represented in Stockholm, and there are reliable local firms as well. You can hire a car at Arlanda Airport when you arrive – or ask for a list at your hotel or travel bureau. You'll find addresses are also listed in the business telephone directory (*Gula Sidorna*) under Biluthyrning.

The legal minimum driving age in Sweden is 18, but to hire a car you usually need to have held a licence for three years, so in practice the minimum age is 21. You'll need your driving licence and passport. Most companies require a deposit, but this is waived if you present an accepted credit card.

I'd like to hire a car.	**Jag skulle vilja hyra en bil.**
a day/a week	**en day/en vecka**
driving licence	**körkort**

CLIMATE and CLOTHING

Most of Sweden has a continental climate, with a medium to large temperature difference between summer and winter. In summer temperatures do rise above 20°C (70°F). Summer is, of course, the prime season to visit Stockholm. In midsummer, daylight lasts up to 19 hours, with lots of sunshine – and lots of other visitors. In spring, which is particularly lovely in the lake district and outlying regions, and autumn, with bright colours and clear nights, you'll have Sweden to yourself. Winter is tempting for sports enthusiasts and Christmas in Sweden can be an unforgettable experience.

The following chart will give you an idea of the average daily maximum and minimum temperatures, and average number of rainy days each month in Stockholm.

	J	F	M	A	M	J	J	A	S	O	N	D
Max °F	31	31	37	45	57	65	70	66	58	48	38	33
Min	23	22	26	32	41	49	55	53	46	39	31	26
Max °C	-1	-1	3	7	14	18	21	19	14	9	3	1
Min	-5	-6	-3	0	5	9	13	12	8	4	-1	-3
Days of rainfall	10	7	6	7	7	8	9	10	9	9	10	11

Clothing. Although the weather is often ideal in the summer – pleasantly warm with low humidity – evenings can be a bit cool, requiring a sweater or shawl. In spring and autumn a light overcoat or raincoat will come in handy, and of course winter requires warm boots and coats, according to your planned activities.

Stockholmers no longer dress up as they used to, and even at the theatre, concert or opera, casual, but smart, clothes are the rule. There are a few late-opening restaurants that require (or expect) guests to wear a tie and jacket.

You should certainly bring appropriate shoes for walking if you're planning to visit the Old Town and city parks. Hiking clothes include sturdy boots, a warm sweater and waterproof clothing.

COMMUNICATIONS (See also TIME DIFFERENCES on p.123)

Unlike certain other European countries the post office only handles mail; for telephone and telegram or telex services you have to go to the Tele offices (see below).

Post Office (*postkontor*). The main post office is not far from the Central Railway Station at Vasagatan 28-34. Stamps and aerogrammes can be bought either at the post office or at tobacco shops, kiosks, department stores and hotels. You'll find a yellow sign with a blue horn outside every post office. Letterboxes are also yellow.

Post offices are open Monday-Friday 9am-6pm. The main office keeps longer hours and is open weekdays 7am-9pm and Saturday 10am-1pm, but closed on Sunday.

To receive your mail poste restante (general delivery) have it sent to the Central Post Office, Stockholm 1.

Telephone (*telefon*), **Telegrams and Faxes**. All phones have fully automatic dialling systems and are conveniently located in glass-enclosed sidewalk stalls and in Tele offices (see below). There are no public telephones at the post offices, but you will find them in some restaurants, bars and shops. Apart from the old coin-operated phones, there are now public telephones that you can operate with credit cards. These are identified by a 'CCC' sign. There are also phones that take disposable telephone cards, which can be purchased at Telia shops, Pressbyrån and various kiosks. They cost 30-90kr.

Dialling instructions are in Swedish and English. You can dial direct to most cities in Europe and the USA. To call the UK from Sweden dial the prefix 00944; for the USA it's 0091 from Stockholm. Reduced rates apply to the USA and Canada from 10pm to 10am, and all day Sunday. For overseas information call 07977. Calls from these phones are cheaper than making a call from your hotel. Within Europe calls cost about 7kr a minute. The minimum cost of a local call is 2kr.

Public telephone and telegraph offices (marked 'Tele') offer fax as well as telegram and telephone services. The main office in Stockholm, open daily from early morning until midnight, is located at Skeppsbron 2. You can also send a telegram by phoning 0021. Most hotels will also be equipped to send faxes.

airmail	**flygpost**
special delivery	**express**
poste restante	**poste restante**
registered	**rekommenderat**
Can you help me get this number?	**Kan ni hjälpa mig att komma till det här numret?**

COMPLAINTS

The Swedish sense of fair play makes complaining a rare event. In a restaurant or hotel, a quiet word with the manager is usually enough.

Serious complaints about hotels or other major services should be directed to tourist offices or to the appropriate travel authority.

CRIME (See also EMERGENCIES on p.111 and POLICE on p.121)

Sweden is one of the safest countries in the world. Nevertheless, like other cities, Stockholm has kept up with the times, which means that crime has increased. You're not likely to get mugged or have your purse snatched, but certain parts of the city, such as parks like Humlegården, can be a bit dangerous – or very unpleasant – late at night. It's a good idea to check your valuables into the hotel safe. Don't leave cameras and packages in view in your car, even if it's locked.

Any loss or theft should be reported at once to the nearest police station – if only for insurance purposes. Your insurance company will need to see a copy of the police report.

I want to report a theft.   **Jag vill anmäla en stöld.**

CUSTOMS and ENTRY FORMALITIES (*tull*)

Visitors from EU countries need only an identity card to enter Sweden. Citizens of most other countries must be in posession of a valid passport. European and North American residents are not subject to any health requirements. In case of doubt, check with Swedish representatives in your own country before departure.

Duty-free allowance. As Sweden is part of the European Union, free exchange of non duty-free goods for personal use is permitted between Sweden and the UK and the Republic of Ireland. However, duty-free items are still subject to restrictions; check before you go. Non-EU country residents returning home may bring back the following duty-free amounts: **Australia**: 250 cigarettes or 250g tobacco, 1l alcohol; **Canada**: 200 cigarettes and 50 cigars and 400g tobacco, 1.1l spirits or wine or 8.5l beer; **New Zealand**: 200 cigarettes or 50 cigars or 250g tobacco, 4.5l wine or beer and 1.1l spirits; **South Africa**: 400 cigarettes and 50 cigars and 250g tobacco, 2l wine and 1l spirits; **USA**: 200 cigarettes and 100 cigars and 2kg tobacco, 1l wine or spirits.

Currency restrictions. There is no restriction on the amount of foreign or local currency you may bring into or take out of the country as a tourist (provided it is declared upon entry).

I have nothing to declare.	**Jag har inget att förtulla.**
It's for my personal use.	**Det är för mitt personliga bruk.**

D

DRIVING IN SWEDEN (See also Car Hire/Rental on p.104)

Swedish roads are well maintained and uncrowded, and outside the cities driving is easy, despite the small number of motorways. If you are taking a car into Sweden you will need:

- a valid national, international driving permit or pink European Union licence
- car registration papers
- Green Card (an extension to your regular insurance policy making it valid for Sweden) or some other internationally valid third party insurance
- national identity sticker.

Driving conditions. Drive on the right, pass on the left. Traffic on main roads and very often main streets in town has right-of-way. Traffic on roundabouts usually has priority, but in other situations traffic from the right has right-of-way. You must also give way to anyone on a pedestrian crossing and to any cyclist who is crossing a cycle track.

It is obligatory for everyone in the car to use seat belts, and that includes back-seat passengers if the car is so equipped. Children under seven should be secured in the back seat with a harness or in a child seat. Note that all vehicles (including motorcycles) must have dipped headlights switched on at all times, even in broad daylight.

Routine spot checks to inspect driving licences and the condition of vehicles are common in Sweden. Drinking and driving is a very serious offence in this country. The police are free to stop motorists and breathalyze them whenever they want to. You can be fined or even sent to jail if your alcohol level exceeds 0.2 per mille.

Most Swedish roads are very good, though only a small proportion are motorways (expressways). Smaller roads, of course, will give you a much better chance to see and appreciate Sweden's unspoiled environment.

Speed limits. Maximum speed limits are indicated by signs on all roads. On principal motorways (expressways) passenger vehicles can usually drive up to 110kmh (70 mph) – or 70kmh (43mph) for a car towing a trailer. On other main roads outside built-up areas the speed limit is 90kmh (55mph) or 70kmh (43mph), depending on road width and traffic density. In towns it is 50kmh (30mph).

Fuel and oil. There are numerous petrol stations, which are mostly self-service. Many stations also have automatic pumps where you can fill up round-the-clock (all you may find open in the evening). These pumps work with 10 and 100 kronor notes and are indicated by the signs *Nattöppet* and *Sedelautomat*. Most petrol stations take credit cards and many of them have shops stocking basic foods, as well as selling newspapers and confectionery.

Parking. In Stockholm parking meters indicate parking areas (parking fines are high). There are also multi-level car parks scattered about the city. On main roads out of town parking is prohibited, but there are many lay-bys arranged for picnicking. A circular sign with a red cross tells you where parking is prohibited. If the restrictions only apply during certain times of the day, the sign will also have a yellow plate with a red border and the times indicated.

Accidents and breakdowns. If you have serious car trouble, you can either contact the police or call Larmtjänst (which is a 24-hour breakdown service), a company owned by the Swedish insurance companies. Their number in Stockholm is 08-24 10 00; otherwise you can ring the following cheap-rate number from anywhere in Sweden: 020-91 00 40. This connects you to the nearest Larmtjänst office. Most of the bigger petrol stations also have motor-mechanics on duty during the day. In the case of serious accidents, especially if **109**

there are injuries, you are justified in making use of the 90-000 emergency telephone number for the police.

Road signs. Most road signs in Sweden are represented as international pictographs, but here are some written ones that you may also see and need to understand:

Biljettautomat	Ticket machine
Bussfil	Bus lane
Busshållplats	Bus-stop
Ej genomfart	No through traffic
Kör sakta	Slow down
Lämna företräde	Give way
Omkörning förbjuden	No overtaking (no passing)
Privat parkering	Private parking
Trafikomläggning	Diversion (detour)
Vägarbete	Roadworks

driving licence	**körkort**
car registration papers	**besiktningsinstrument**
Please check the oil/tyres/battery.	**Kan ni kontrollera oljan/däcken/batteriet, tack.**
I have had a breakdown.	**Bilen har gått sonder.**
There's been an accident.	**Det har hänt en olycka.**

Distance

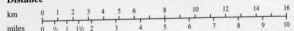

Fluid measures

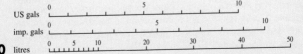

litres

ELECTRIC CURRENT

The supply for electric appliances in Sweden is 220 volt, 50 Hz AC, and requires standard two-pin, round continental plugs. Visitors should bring their own adaptors.

EMBASSIES and CONSULATES (*ambassad; konsulat*)

Most of the embassies are open 8am-4pm, but there is usually a 24-hour service. Telephone in advance if in doubt. The following are some of the embassies and consulates in Stockholm:

Australia: *Embassy*: Sergels Torg 12, 103 86 Stockholm; tel. 08-613 29 60.

Canada: *Embassy*: Tegelbacken 4, 103 23 Stockholm; tel. 08-613 99 00.

Republic of Ireland: *Consulate*: Östermalmsgatan 97, S-114-69 Stockholm; tel. 08-661 80 05/08-661 74 09.

UK: *Embassy with consular section*: Skarpögatan 6-8, 11527 Stockholm; tel. 08-667 01 40.

USA: *Embassy with consular section*: Strandvägen 101, 115 89 Stockholm; tel. 08-783 53 00.

EMERGENCIES (See also POLICE on p.121 and MEDICAL CARE on p.116)

Radio Sweden broadcasts vital messages to travellers in Sweden. The station can be heard on medium wave 1179KHz (254m), and in the Stockholm area on FM 89.6MHz, and messages should be sent to a broadcasting organization in your country of origin, Interpol, or the appropriate embassy in Sweden (see EMBASSIES AND CONSULATES above, and see also MEDIA on p.115).

The general emergency telephone number in Sweden is 90-000. This number covers the police and fire departments, ambulance and medical services. It can be dialled free (no coins needed) from any telephone. English is usually understood.

| Help! | **Hjälp!** |
| There's been an accident. | **Det har hänt en olycka.** |

ENVIRONMENTAL ISSUES

You may be tempted to buy exotic souvenirs for yourself and your family on your holiday, but spare a thought for endangered plants and animals that may be threatened by your purchase. Even trade in tourist souvenirs can threaten the most endangered species.

Over 800 species of animals and plants are currently banned from international trade by CITES (Convention on International Trade in Endangered Species and Plants). These include many corals, shells, cacti, orchids and hardwoods, as well as the more obvious tigers, rhinos, spotted cats and turtles.

So think twice before you buy – it may be illegal and your souvenirs could be confiscated by Customs on your return.

For further information or a fact sheet contact the following:

UK: Department of the Environment; tel. (01179) 878 961 (birds, reptiles and fish), or (01179) 878 168 (plants and mammals).

US: Fish and Wildlife Service; tel. (001) 703 358 2095; fax (001) 703 358 2281.

GAY and LESBIAN TRAVELLERS

Sweden is one of the world's most progressive countries when it comes to Gay Rights. Since 1988 government legislation has granted gay relationships the same status as heterosexual marriages and the state has given financial support to gay organizations. Information and advice can be obtained from the Swedish Federation for Lesbian and Gay Rights: RSFL (Riksförbundet för Sexuellt Likaberättigade), Stockholms Gay-hus, Sveavägen 57. (Postal address: Förbundskansli, Box 350, S-101-26 Stockholm); tel. 08-736 02 13.

GUIDES and TOURS (guide)

The Swedish Tourist Board and the Stockholm Information Service can recommend excursions and trips. Sightseeing buses and boats have multilingual guides, and there are also guided tours in some museums. Authorized guides can be booked by ringing 08-789 24 31 any day of the week.

I'd like an English-speaking guide.	**Jag skulle vilja ha en guide som talar engelska.**

LANGUAGE

(See also the USEFUL EXPRESSIONS on the cover of this guide)

English is widely spoken and understood all over Sweden, especially in bigger towns. Children study English at school from the age of nine. German is the next choice of language and is spoken by many (particularly in the tourist industry).

Although Swedish is a pleasant language to hear, you are unlikely to find it easy to pronounce. Remember there are three extra letters in the Swedish alphabet – å, ä and ö – which appear after the usual 26 letters (something to bear in mind when looking up a name in the telephone book).

The BERLITZ SWEDISH PHRASE BOOK and DICTIONARY covers practically all the situations you're likely to encounter during your travels in Sweden, while the SWEDISH-ENGLISH/ENGLISH-SWEDISH POCKET DICTIONARY contains some 12,500 concepts and a special menu-reader supplement to help you cope with the most difficult stumbling blocks.

Useful expressions

big/small	**stor/liten**	next/last	**nästa/sista**
quick/slow	**snabb/långsam**	good/bad	**bra/dålig**
hot/cold	**varm/kall**	early/late	**tidig/sen**
heavy/light	**tung/lätt**	cheap/expensive	**billig/dyr**

open/shut	**öpen/stängd**	near/far	**nära/långt**
right/wrong	**rätt/fel**		**(bort)**
old/new	**gammal/ny**	here/there	**här/där**

Days of the week

Sunday	**söndag**	Thursday	**torsdag**
Monday	**måndag**	Friday	**fredag**
Tuesday	**tisdag**	Saturday	**lördag**
Wednesday	**onsdag**		

Numbers

0	**noll**	11	**elva**	30	**trettio**
1	**ett**	12	**tolv**	40	**fyrtio**
2	**två**	13	**tretton**	50	**femtio**
3	**tre**	14	**fjorton**	60	**sextio**
4	**fyra**	15	**femton**	70	**sjuttio**
5	**fem**	16	**sexton**	80	**åttio**
6	**sex**	17	**sjutton**	90	**nittio**
7	**sju**	18	**arton**	100	**(ett)hundra**
8	**åtta**	19	**nitton**	101	**hundraett**
9	**nio**	20	**tjugo**	110	**hundratio**
10	**tio**	21	**tjugoett**	1000	**(ett)tusen**

LAUNDRY and DRY CLEANING (*tvätt; kemtvätt*)

You can get quick service in the hotels and in certain laundry or dry-cleaning establishments, but prices are high, especially for dry cleaning. If you have a lot of laundry, take it to a self-service launderette (*Ivättonmat* or *Tvättbar*). For addresses look for 'Kemisk Tvätt' or 'Tvättbarer' in the business phone book (*Gula Sidorna*).

When will it be ready?	**När kan det bli klart?**
I need it tomorrow morning.	**Jag måste ha det i morgon bitti.**

LOST PROPERTY (hittegods)

The main lost property office (hittegodsexpedition) is at the police station at Tjärhovsgatan 21 (tel. 08-769 30 75) in Stockholm, open Monday to Friday from 9am to 12 noon and from 1pm to 5pm. Taxi drivers deliver lost articles to this office.

For articles lost on buses and underground trains, contact the Stockholm Local Traffic Office (SL) at the Rådmansgatan underground station, Monday to Friday from 11am to 4pm (Thursday 5-7pm); tel. 08-600 10 00.

I've lost my
handbag/passport/wallet.

Jag har tappat min handväska/mitt pass/min plånbok.

MEDIA

Radio and Television. Sveriges Radio (Radio Sweden) and Sveriges Television (Swedish Broadcasting Corporation) used to have a monopoly on all radio and television programmes transmitted in Sweden. Now, however, there are also privately owned radio stations and television channels. Sveriges Radio broadcasts regular 30-minute programmes of news and information in English, which can be heard over most of Sweden on medium wave 1179KHz (254m), and also in the Stockholm area on FM 89.6MHz. Further details are available from Radio Sweden International, S-105-10 Stockholm, tel. 08-784 00, or from many hotels. Two of the country's five TV channels are financed through licence fees, while the others accept advertisements. News in English is broadcast in summer. For the schedule, refer to the local papers. In addition to Swedish channels, most hotels carry English-language satellite channels such as Super Channel and CNN, plus German-language channels direct from Germany.

Newspapers and Magazines (*tidning; tidskrift*). Sweden's main daily newspapers are *Svenska Dagbladet*, *Dagens Nyheter* and *Göteborgs Posten* (these are broadsheets), and *Expressen* and *Aftonbladet* (these are tabloids), all in Swedish. The *International Herald Tribune* and leading English papers, as well as a wide variety of magazines, are sold at the Central Railway Station, airport shops, hotels, tobacco shops and kiosks in central Stockholm.

The Stockholm Information Service publish a guide to what's happening around the capital, called *Stockholm This Week*. This is usually available free from your hotel.

Where can I buy an English language newspaper?	**Var kan jag köpa en engelskspråkig tidning?**

MEDICAL CARE (See also EMERGENCIES on p.111)

No vaccinations are needed for entry to Sweden. In the case of British subjects – and citizens of most other European countries – Sweden's national health insurance plan covers any illness or accident that requires doctors' services or hospitalization. This is due to a reciprocal agreement between the two countries. If you are not British you should check to see if your private insurance covers medical treatment in Sweden before leaving home.

If you fall ill, have an accident, or are in need of a doctor, ask someone such as your hotel receptionist to call a doctor for you. Make sure the doctor is affiliated to Försäktringskassan (Swedish Natioal Health Service). If you are able, go to a hospital's emergency and casualty reception (*akutmottagning*) or to City-Akuten, at Holländargatan 3; tel. 08-11 71 77. Take your passport with you for identification. Hospital visits cost 90kr, and 200kr if you have to be attended by the casualty department. Any prescriptions need to be taken to a chemist (*spotek*).

Dental treatment. A dental surgery is called *tandläkare* in Swedish. For emergency dental treatment go to the clinic called Akuttandvärden at St Eriks Sjukhus, Fleminggatan 22, 11282 Stockholm; tel. 08-54 11 17 (8am-7pm, telephone calls up to 9pm). Alternatively, you can telephone Sjukvärdsupplysningen on 08-44 92 00, a 24-hour service that will put you in touch with a dentist.

Chemists/Pharmacies (*apotek*). They stock over-the-counter products like cough medicine or aspirin and also supply prescriptions. A 24-hour pharmacy service is offered by C W Scheele at Klarabergsgatan 64 (near the Central Station); tel. 08-24 82 80. Nevertheless, it is a good idea to bring along an adequate supply of any prescribed medication from home.

Can you get me a doctor?	**Kan ni skaffa mig en läkare?**
Where is the nearest (all-night) pharmacy?	**Var ligger närmaste (jour)apotek?**

MONEY MATTERS

Currency. Sweden's monetary unit is the *krona* or crown (plural *kronor*), abbreviated kr, or abroad Skr, to distinguish it from the Danish and Norwegian kronor. It is divided into 100 *öre*. (For currency restrictions, see CUSTOMS AND ENTRY FORMALITIES on p.107)

Silver coins: 50 öre, 1 krona, 5 and 10 kronor.

Banknotes: 20, 100, 500, 1,000 and 10,000 kronor.

Banks and currency exchange. Foreign currency can be changed in practically all commercial and savings banks, and the larger hotels and department stores. You get a better rate of exchange for banknotes and traveller's cheques in banks or exchange offices, of course. The bank at Arlanda airport and the exchange bureau (*växelkontor*) at the Central Railway Station are open every day until evening. (See also OPENING HOURS on p.120)

Credit cards and traveller's cheques. Most of the international credit cards are welcome – shops and restaurants usually display signs indicating the ones they accept. Traveller's cheques can be cashed at the bank or at your hotel.

VAT/sales tax. This is called *Moms* in Sweden, and is 25% on all goods and on most services (12% for accommodation). *Moms* will be refunded in cash at any point of departure to visitors who have made purchases in shops displaying the blue-and-yellow 'Tax-Free Shopping' sticker. You should present your passport at the time of **117**

purchase. Later, simply hand over the Tax-Free Shopping Cheque provided by the shop (be sure to fill out the back), at the Tax-Free Service counter in ports, airports and aboard ships. This refund is available only for a limited period after purchase, and is only open to non-Scandinavian residents.

Stockholm Card (*Stockholmskortet*). This offers you the chance to see the city at a reasonable price. Similar in appearance to a credit card, it allows the holder free entry to about 60 museums, castles and other sights, free public transport, including sightseeing buses and boats, reduced-price excursions to Drottningholm Palace, free parking (provided a special parking card is obtained at the time of purchase) and more. Used to the full, the card represents a considerable bargain. The pass is valid from one to three days. It is available only through local tourist offices such as those at Sweden House and the Central Station (see TOURIST INFORMATION OFFICES on p.123). Another version is available without the sightseeing concessions.

| I'd like to change some dollars/pounds. | **Jag skulle vilja växla några dollar/pund.** |

Planning your budget

The following are some prices in Swedish kronor (kr). However, remember that all these prices must be regarded as approximate and cannot account for inflation.

Car hire. Prices vary tremendously. Small car (VW Golf): weekend, including 200km (140 miles), 600kr; week (5-7 days), including 1,000km (700 miles), 3,000kr. Large car (SAAB 9,000 CDE): weekend, including 200km (140 miles), 1,000kr; week (5-7 days), including 1,000km (700 miles), 5,000kr. Each extra km costs 1kr. If you hire a car for a weekend, this means you have it from noon on Friday to noon on Monday.

Guides. These are not cheap: around 650kr for three hours, and 200kr or more for each additional hour, plus booking fee of 150kr.

Hotels. Average rates for hotels (per night) can be divided into three categories (based on two people sharing a double room and including full breakfast): under 1,100kr; 1,100-1,800kr; over 1,800kr. Prices at the lower end may be well below 1,100kr – but, equally, prices at the top end may rise considerably above 1,800kr. These are full rates. Visitors can take advantage of weekend, special and summer rates and packages. (See also ACCOMMODATION on p.100 and the list of Recommended Hotels starting on p.65)

Meals and drinks. Continental breakfast in a restaurant/café costs 50kr; lunch 60-70kr; dinner at a medium-priced restaurant (not including drinks) 200kr per head. Coffee or soft drinks cost 15kr; a bottle of wine 100kr and up; spirits (4cl) 70kr, except aquavit (4cl) 50kr. Look out for the sign *Dagens rätt* (dish of the day) – salad, a main course and coffee – which is usually good value.

Museums. The cost is 10-50kr, an average 30kr. (Some are free.)

Petrol. It costs 7.70-8.10kr per litre and diesel costs about 5.75kr. There are petrol stations with automatic 24-hour pumps that take 100kr notes.

Public transport. A single ticket for the bus/*tunnelbana*/local train is 13kr.

Self-catering. Food and (especially) alcoholic drinks are expensive. Self-caterers are advised to bring in a car-load of food and other necessities with them.

Stockholm Card (*Stockholmskort*). The basic 24-hour card costs 150kr, the 72-hour card 450kr. Also available is the Stockholm Tourist Card, offering unlimited free travel on public transport within the Greater Stockholm area but no sightseeing concessions. The cost is 56kr for 24 hours, 107kr for 72 hours.

Taxis. Basic charge 45-70kr within the city area. Some Stockholm taxis have a set fare of 75kr within the Stockholm city boundaries.

Trains. A single journey between Stockholm and Gothenburg, 2nd class 394kr. Single sleeper journey from Stockholm to Kiruna 2nd class, rail ticket 594kr plus sleeper 155-855kr, depending on the facilities available.

Video. To rent a video camera costs 400kr for 24 hours, plus *Moms*. The cost of a 3-hour cassette tape is 40kr.

OPENING HOURS (See also Public Holidays on p.121)

Shops and department stores are usually open weekdays from 9 or 9.30am to 6pm, Saturdays until 3 or 4pm. Some of the bigger department stores stay open later on weekdays and are open on Sunday afternoons. Food shops have the same hours, but some supermarkets in major underground (subway) stations keep later hours and also open on Sunday afternoons. Certain food shops, *närbutiker*, are open every day of the year from either 7am to 11pm, or 10am to 10pm.

Post offices are generally open Monday to Friday from 9am to 6pm. The main post office in Stockholm is open weekdays 7am to 9pm, Saturday 10am to 1pm; closed Sundays.

Banks are open Monday to Friday from 9.30am to 3pm (some open again in the afternoon one day a week from 4 to 5.30pm). The bank at Arlanda airport is open daily from 7am to 10pm, and the Exchange Bureau at the Central Railway Station from 8am to 9pm.

Museums are usually open from 10 or 11am to 4pm. (See also the list of Museums starting on p.46)

Chemists/pharmacies are open during normal shopping hours; a number stay open on duty at night and on Sundays. (See Medical Care on p.116)

P

PHOTOGRAPHY and VIDEO (*fotografering*)

All popular types of camera and film are available in Sweden at good prices – in fact, cameras are a very good buy. Video tapes and equipment are also widely available.

Colour film development usually takes one week, although a number of shops in the centre of town offer either a one-hour or two-day service. You should be aware that photographic film is expensive. A

36-exposure transparency film can cost 100-120kr. However, there are bargains to be found, so you should shop around.

Some museums allow visitors to take photos, but never with a tripod or flash. For handy tips on how to get the most out of your holiday photographs, purchase a copy of the Berlitz-Nikon POCKET GUIDE TO TRAVEL PHOTOGRAPHY (available in the UK only).

I'd like a film for this camera.	**Jag skulle vilja ha en film till den här kameran.**
black-and-white film	**svartvit film**
colour prints	**färgfilm**
colour slides	**färgfilm för diabilder**
How long will it take to develop this film?	**Hur lång tid tar det att framkalla den här filmen?**

POLICE (*polis*)
(See also CRIME on p.107 and EMERGENCIES on p.111)

The Stockholm police patrol cars are marked 'Polis'. Members of the force are invariably courteous and helpful to tourists, and all of them speak some English, so don't hesitate to ask them questions or directions. Police headquarters is at Agnegatan 33-37 in Stockholm; tel. 08-769 30 00. The emergency police number (also fire, ambulance, etc) is 90-000; no money is required from a pay phone.

There are meter maids, dressed in light-blue uniforms, who check the time limits on the parking of cars and issue parking tickets for violations of the restrictions (they do a thorough job). On the motorways and roads the police often carry out routine spot checks.

Where's the police station?	**Var ligger polisstationen?**

PUBLIC HOLIDAYS (*helgdag*)

Banks, offices and shops close on public holidays in Sweden, as do most restaurants, museums, food shops and tourist attractions. Note that many establishments also close early on the day before a holiday – some may even close for the entire day beforehand. On Christmas Eve virtually everything is closed.

1 January	*Nyårsdagen*	New Year's Day
6 January	*Trettondagen*	Twelfth Day
1 May	*Första Maj*	May Day
Sat between 20 and 26 June	*Midsommardagen*	Midsummer Day
Sat between 31 Oct and 6 Nov	*Allhelgonadagen*	All Saints' Day
24 December	*Julafton*	Christmas Eve
25 December	*Juldagen*	Christmas Day
26 December	*Annandag jul*	Boxing Day

Movable Dates

late March/ early April	*Långfredagen*	Good Friday
late March/ early April	*Påskdagen/ Annandag påsk*	Easter/ Easter Monday
May	*Kristi himmelsfärds-dag*	Ascension Day
May	*Pingstdagen/ Annandag pingst*	Whit Sunday/ Monday

RELIGION

About 95% of Sweden's native-born population are Lutheran Evangelical, the state-established church. Roman Catholics are estimated at about 60,000 and those of Jewish and other faiths are also represented. Non-Lutheran services are held in the following churches (services are on Sunday at 11am):

Anglican: Anglican Church, Strandvägen 76; tel. 08-661 22 23.

Catholic: Marie Bebådelsekyrkan (The Church of the Blessed Annunciation), Linnégatan 79; tel. 08-661 69 36.

Jewish: The Great Synagogue (conservative), Wahrendorffsgatan 3A; tel. 08-23 51 60.

TIME DIFFERENCES

Sweden follows Central European Time (GMT + 1). In summer, the Swedes put their clocks ahead one hour. The following chart shows times across the world in summer:

New York	London	Paris	**Stockholm**	Sydney	Auckland
6am	11am	noon	**noon**	8pm	10pm

TIPPING

Service charges are included in hotel and restaurant bills. Gratuities for waiters, hotel maids, tourist guides, and many others in the tourist-related industries, are purely optional. Obviously, a little extra is appreciated for special services rendered, but it isn't expected. In some areas, however, the habit may be more engrained:

Cloakroom attendant	charges posted or 5kr
Hairdresser/Barber	optional
Hotel porter, per bag	3-4kr (optional)
Taxi driver	tip included in bill

TOILETS (*toalett*)

Public facilities are located in some underground (subway) stations, department stores and some of the bigger streets, squares and parks. They are often labelled with symbols for men and women, or marked WC, *Damer/Herrar* (Ladies/Gentlemen) or simply D/H. Some have slots for coins or an attendant to give towels and soap. The usual charge is 5kr.

TOURIST INFORMATION OFFICES

In Sweden tourist offices (*turistbyrå*) are indicated by the international sign (a white 'i' on a green background). There are more than 300 non-profit tourist offices around the country. They stock a good selection of brochures and maps (*karta*) of their respective regions, **123** and can provide you with information on sightseeing, excursions, restaurants, hotels, camping, sports, etc.

In Stockholm the main place to go is Sweden House (Sverige-huset), Hamngatan 27, near Kungsträdgarden, Box 7542, 10393 Stockholm; tel. 08-789 24 95. This groups several tourist organizations at the same address and telephone number, including the offices of the Stockholm Information Service, the Tourist Centre, providing information on Stockholm and surrounding areas, the Swedish Institute (Svenska Institutet), a currency exchange office, a library and a bookshop with information about Sweden in foreign languages, open on weekdays.

Hotellcentralen, Stockholm's official accommodation service, has branches at the Central Railway Station (lower ground floor), tel. 08-24 08 80, and at Arlanda airport.

The Swedish Travel and Tourism Council also has representatives in the following countries:

UK: Swedish Travel and Tourism Council, 73 Welbeck Street, **London** W1M 8AN; tel. (0171) 935-9784.

USA: Scandinavian National Tourist Offices, 655 Third Avenue, 18th floor, **New York**, NY 10017; tel. (212) 949-2333.

Scandinavian Tourist Board, Denmark-Sweden, 150 North Michigan Avenue, Suite 2110, **Chicago**, IL 60601; tel. (312) 899-1121.

Scandinavian Tourist Board, Denmark-Sweden, 8929 Wilshire Boulevard, Suite 300, **Beverly Hills**, CA 90211; tel. (213) 854-1549.

TRANSPORT

Bus and underground/subway. Stockholm has very efficient and modern underground or subway (*tunnelbana*) and bus systems which make it easy to get around the city and its environs from about 5am (a little later on Sundays) to 2am. Underground stations are indicated by a blue 'T'. There are maps for the underground in the station and on the train. Stockholm's bus network is the largest in the world, and is run by the Stockholm Transit Authority, which also operates integrated underground and local train services.

Tickets are valid on all these means of transport for one hour from the time they are stamped. They can be bought from bus drivers, at underground station booths or at Press Agency (*Pressbyrån*) newsstands in cards of 18 units, which are stamped according to the distance travelled. Children and pensioners (senior citizens) only have to pay half-price.

Special one-day and three-day tourist tickets are also sold in the Pressbyrån kiosks.

Tourist buses. These also circulate between the major attractions.

Taxis. You can flag taxis down anywhere in Stockholm, or find them at stands marked 'Taxi' (the biggest is in front of the Central Railway Station). The sign *Ledig* (vacant) lighted up indicates when a taxi is available. However, cabs are difficult to find during rush hours and on rainy days. If you want to book one in advance call 08-15 04 00 or ask your hotel receptionist to reserve one for you.

Some taxis belong to a cooperative that sets a fixed fare on certain routes around the capital. They are identifiable by a yellow half moon on the roof, and can offer a considerable saving on standard taxis. (For advice on tipping see TIPPING on p.123)

Trains (*tåg*). Swedish State Railway (Statens Järnvägar or SJ) operates an extensive network of routes, with more than 90% of the traffic carried on electric trains. It's a reliable railway system, with trains leaving Stockholm for most big towns every hour or two. The new X2000 high-speed trains (which can reach speeds of up to 200kmh/124mph) drastically cut the travelling times between Stockholm and other cities within the country. From the Central Station (Centralstationen) you can reach virtually every part of Sweden by rail, and there are direct links to Copenhagen, Berlin and other European cities. Long-distance trains have restaurant cars and/or buffets, and there are also sleepers and couchettes for both first- and second-class travel.

Fares are based on a 'sliding scale' – the longer the journey, the lower the price per kilometre. Children under 6 travel free. Seat reservations are often compulsory, especially on express trains (*expresståg*). Enquire about the various discount plans available. You can buy a wanderlust card (*reslustkort*) that allows you half-price, second-class rail travel on certain trains, and other cost-cutting benefits. It is valid for one year and costs 250kr. On some trains, marked 'R' or 'IC', you must reserve a seat (price 20kr), which can be done right up to the time of departure.

Inter-city coaches (*snabbussar*). Express buses can be used instead of (or in addition to) trains to many places in Sweden. Although there are private companies, Swedish Railways operates a low-priced, efficient coach system between towns, cities and outlying areas. For schedules and bookings check with the office at Cityterminalen, tel. 08-23 71 90. Branch offices for state-run coach and rail services are indicated by the sign *SJ Resebyrå*, and tickets can be purchased in any railway station.

Boat excursions. Stockholm and its environs are made to order for boat excursions. Sightseeing boats cruise under the city's bridges, steamers serve the islands of the archipelago in the Baltic and ply the waters of Lake Mälaren, making stops at Drottningholm Palace, Gripsholm Castle and other noteworthy places. Tours range from a one-hour trip in the city to a long cruise with a stay overnight in Sandhamn on the island of Sandön. Private companies offer a wide choice of excursions, which you will find listed at the Stockholm Information Service (see TOURIST INFORMATION OFFICES on p.123).

Yachting. If you are a seasoned sailor and would like to rent a boat you should know the regulations that apply to Swedish territorial waters, and where guest harbours are located. Get in touch with the Swedish Touring Club (STF): Box 25, Drottninggatan 31-33, 101 20 Stockholm; tel. 08-790 31 00.

single (one way)	**enkel**
return (round trip)	**tur och retur**

TRAVELLERS WITH DISABILITIES

Facilities for disabled people include access ramps, lifts, and hotel rooms adapted for people with mobility difficulties or allergies, good public transport access, and special provisions for swimming and riding. Almost all pedestrian crossings use sound to indicate when it is safe to cross. For further information contact Sweden's National Council for the Disabled:

Statens Handikapprådd, Regeringsgatan 567, S-103-96 Stockholm; tel. 08-787 73 20.

The disabled can obtain information about accommodation that has been adapted to suit their needs from the Swedish 'Hotels Guide', and there is an English-language *Holiday Guide for the Disabled* that is available from the Swedish Travel and Tourist Council.

TRAVELLING TO STOCKHOLM

Because of the complexity and variability of the many fares, you should ask the advice of an informed travel agent well before your departure.

By air

Scheduled flights

Stockholm's Arlanda airport (see AIRPORTS on p.101), the main gateway to Sweden, is linked by regular flights from numerous European and several North American cities. A connecting service for cities throughout Europe and from North America and the Middle East and Far East operates via Copenhagen Airport. The flight from London to Stockholm takes approximately 2½ hours, from New York to Stockholm 10½ hours.

Charter flights and package tours

From the UK and Ireland: Charter flights and package tours to Sweden are highly uncommon. Within Sweden, however, there are a number of attractive packages – ask for up-to-date information at a reliable travel agency when you arrive, as the types of tickets are constantly changing.

127

From North America: Stockholm is featured on GITs (Group Inclusive Tours) of 15 days or longer. Some tours offer two days of visits in the city before a boat trip through the Norwegian Fjords. Several packages are available to Scandinavia plus Lappland and the North Cape. GIT includes round-trip air transport, hotel accommodation, specified meals, transfers, baggage handling, ground transport, service charges, taxes and an English-speaking guide.

For visitors from North America and the Far East there is also the advantageous Visit Scandinavia plan – enquire at a travel agency before leaving home.

By sea and road

Many people find the ferry services to Sweden inexpensive and comfortable. You can travel with or without your car from the UK ports of Harwich or Newcastle to Gothenburg. The journey lasts about 24 hours, but book in advance, especially for summer crossings. Your car must be on the quay at least one hour before sailing time.

The E20 (formerly E3) is the most direct route from Gothenburg to Stockholm, but you can also follow smaller scenic roads on the way. Various package holidays, generally designed for motorists, include the boat trip plus all sorts of accommodation, from camping and cabins to hotels. Those travelling without a car can make connections from Gothenburg by train. Other inexpensive means of travel are express buses, postal cars and Swedish Railways' inter-city weekend bus service.There is a coach service between London and Stockholm every day in summer and three days a week for the rest of the year. The journey takes 47 hours.

The main access route from continental Europe is by car ferry from Puttgarden on the north German island of Fehmarn, to Rødbyhavn on the Danish island of Lolland. Then continue through Denmark, via Copenhagen, to Elsinore (Helsingør) for another ferry crossing to Helsingborg in Sweden, and take the E4 to Stockholm. Another possibility is to take the 12-hour car-ferry from Kiel in northern Germany to Gothenburg in Sweden and drive the 520km (320 miles) to Stockholm. Other ferry crossings between north Germany and Sweden are Travemünde-Trelleborg or Malmö.

By rail

You can travel from London to Stockholm by train via the Harwich-Hook (Holland) crossing or Dover-Ostend, then on to Sweden by way of Copenhagen (Hook-Stockholm takes 22-25 hours, Ostend-Gothenburg-Stockholm 26-28 hours). From London it is also possible to travel (with your car) in Le Shuttle channel tunnel to Paris, from where you can continue your journey by road.

The main rail route from continental Europe is the Lübeck-Puttgarden-Rødbyhavn-Copenhagen stretch (see above for an outline of this route).

The Inter-Rail Card is valid for one month's unlimited second-class travel in Europe for young people under 26, for whom there are also discount fares. The Rail Europ Senior card, obtainable before departure only, entitles senior citizens to purchase train tickets for European destinations at reduced prices.

People living outside Europe and North Africa can purchase a Eurailpass for unlimited travel in 16 European countries, including Sweden. This pass must be obtained before leaving home.

Within Sweden, visitors can purchase various rail bargains: SJ Sverige-kort (Sweden Card) permits first- and second-class travel at a discount that varies according to the day of travel, for a period of one year. Finally, the Nordic Tourist Ticket allows unlimited travel on Swedish and other Scandinavian trains for 21 days (and 50% discount on boats to Finland and the island of Åland). There are also some rail tours with unlimited stopovers, including Stockholm.

WATER (vatten)

Water from the tap is perfectly safe to drink anywhere in Sweden. If you prefer mineral water, however, you'll find the local brands excellent and readily available. In remote mountain areas you can drink sparkling water straight from the lake or brook.

WEIGHTS AND MEASURES

For fluid and distance measures, see p.110. Sweden uses the metric system. You will find that Swedes use commas instead of full points to indicate decimals and use full points instead of commas to indicate thousands.

Length

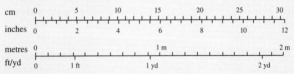

Weight

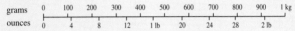

Temperature

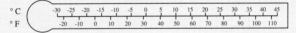

WOMEN TRAVELLERS

Relationships between men and women in Sweden are probably the most 'equal' in the world, and Swedish women organize their own lives freely, enjoying themselves as and when they please.

There are many women's organizations, mostly connected to political parties, but two professional (rather than social) ones are:

Stiftelsen Kvinnor Kan, Östermalmsgatan 33, S-114-26 Stockholm; tel. 08-723 07 07.

Yrkeskvinnors Riksförbund (Federation of Business and Professional Women), Drottninggatan 59 3tr, S-11-21 Stockholm. This organization is affiliated to the International Federation of Business and Professional Women.

YOUTH HOSTELS (*vandrarhem*) (See also MONEY MATTERS on p.117)

Most of the youth hostels in Sweden are located in the southern and central parts of the country. They are cheap, comfortable and open to everyone, irrespective of age. Most have hot and cold water in the rooms and showers, and many have special family rooms suitable for motorists with children under 16. You can bring your own sheets or buy them; sleeping bags are generally not allowed.

Sweden has almost 300 youth hostels, with more than 100 of them open all year. The accommodation is available in a wide range of buildings, from manor houses and former prisons (such as Långholmen in Stockholm) to purpose-built ones. Many of the hostels are in remote areas as well as in towns, catering for all ages and with two-bed, four-bed and family rooms.

Hostels in Sweden are run by Svenska Turistföreningen (Swedish Tourist Club), who offer everything from camping packages and simple mountain cabins, where you provide your own food, to hotel-standard accommodation.

If you are a member of an organization affiliated to the International Youth Hostel Federation, your card is valid in Sweden. All Swedish hostels are listed in the IYHF handbook. For more information on Swedish hostels, contact one of the following:

England: YHA Services, 14 Southampton Street, London WC2E 7HY.

Sweden: Svenska Turistföreningen (Swedish Touring Club), Drottninggatan 31-33, Stockholm; tel. 08-790 32 50.

USA: American Youth Hostels, Inc, National Campus, Delaplane, Virginia 22025.

The SSRS Hotell Domus, a student organization, also operates a hotel service with rooms for rent during summer holidays at very reasonable rates. Their address is Box 5906, Körsbärsvägen 1, 114 89 Stockholm, Sweden, tel. 08-16 01 95. **131**

Index

Where there is more than one set of references, the one in **bold** refers to the main entry. Page numbers in *italic* refer to an illustration.

133

Other Berlitz titles include:

Africa
Kenya
Morocco
South Africa
Tunisia

Asia, Middle East
Bali and Lombok
China
Egypt
Hong Kong
India
Indonesia
Israel
Japan
Malaysia
Singapore
Sri Lanka
Thailand

Australasia
Australia
New Zealand
Sydney

Austria, Switzerland
Austrian Tyrol
Switzerland
Vienna

**Belgium,
The Netherlands**
Amsterdam
Bruges and Ghent
Brussels

British Isles
Channel Islands
Dublin
Edinburgh
Ireland
London
Scotland

**Caribbean,
Latin America**
Bahamas
Bermuda
Cancún and Cozumel

Cuba
French West Indies
Jamaica
Mexico
Puerto Rico
Southern Caribbean
Virgin Islands

**Central and
Eastern Europe**
Budapest
Czech Republic
Moscow and
St Petersburg
Prague

France
Brittany
Côte d'Azur
Dordogne
Euro Disney Resort
France
Normandy
Paris
Provence

Germany
Berlin
Munich

**Greece, Cyprus
and Turkey**
Athens
Corfu
Crete
Cyprus
Greek Islands
Istanbul
Rhodes
Turkey

Italy and Malta
Florence
Italy
Malta
Milan and the Lakes
Naples
Rome
Sicily
Venice

North America
Boston
California
Canada
Disneyland and the
Theme Parks of South-
ern California
Florida
Hawaii
Los Angeles
New Orleans
New York
San Francisco
USA
Walt Disney World
and Orlando
Washington D.C.

Portugal
Algarve
Lisbon
Madeira
Portugal

Scandinavia
Copenhagen
Helsinki
Oslo and Bergen
Stockholm
Sweden

Spain
Barcelona
Canary Islands
Costa Blanca
Costa del Sol
Costa Dorada and
Tarragona
Ibiza and Formentera
Madrid
Mallorca and Menorca
Spain

IN PREPARATION
Channel Hopper's
Wine Guide (UK only)

136

029/610 RP